MW00884105

Close That Loan!

Originating and Processing Residential Real Estate Loan Applications

by

Cheryl L. Peck

authorHOUSE®

AuthorHouse™
1663 Liberty Drive, Suite 200
Bloomington, IN 47403
www.authorhouse.com
Phone: 1-800-839-8640

First published by AuthorHouse 8/27/2008

ISBN: 978-1-4389-0631-7 (sc)

Library of Congress Control Number: 2008906870

Printed in the United States of America
Bloomington, Indiana

This book is printed on acid-free paper.

Every effort has been made to ensure the information presented in this book is accurate and complete as of the date published. Given the volatility of the mortgage industry; laws, regulations and program requirements can and do change frequently. Always check with your lenders, attorneys and broker associations for current information and requirements.

Table of Contents

Introduction

This book is designed to be used by those in the residential real estate financing industry as a quick reference guide to originating and processing residential real estate mortgage loans. Using this book, even novice originators and processors should be able to take a file from initial application to post closing. The methods and tips were developed over my ten-year career as a mortgage broker. I started with a two-day training course on how to originate loans, and knew almost nothing about processing them. In the beginning, I would close one loan a month until I eventually felt confident enough to handle more. During the refinance boom we were closing more than seventy loans per month. I learned the mortgage broker business by trial and error—making and correcting mistakes. I hope this book will help jump-start your career, and allow you to learn from my mistakes! Watch for tips highlighted throughout the book that could save you time and stress.

This book is written from my perspective as a mortgage broker. If you are working directly for a lender, the basic process should be the same. A broker will check with different lenders to determine applicable programs. Working directly for a mortgage banker or lender, you will have access to the programs your employer provides.

There are frequent changes in program guidelines, federal and state laws, lender procedures, and technology. Loan officers and processors should take advantage of training offered by national and state broker associations to keep current.

CHAPTER 1

Organization and Attention to Detail

Originating and processing real estate mortgage loans is not difficult, however, it can be complicated because there are many details about individual programs, and individual lender requirements, as well as federal and state laws involved. After processing several files for the same basic programs and lenders, you will learn the specifics for the programs and lenders you use most. For more uncommon programs, you can look for the information in the guidelines on the lender's web site or ask the lender's underwriter, who approves the loans for the lender. Any information you are not aware of and didn't provide in the file will be requested by the underwriter in the conditions given upon loan approval.

The key to successful originating and processing is communication. Issues and problems can arise on even the simplest file. Make sure everyone involved, including client, seller, real estate agents, and attorneys, are told as soon as possible—especially if the issue will affect the closing date. I always tried to have a solution or alternative to present when I gave the bad news. I found that most people were pretty good about accepting bad news if told early in the process and offered an alternative or solution. I've heard horror stories of processors and loan officers who kept issues quiet, promising a closing date they knew was impossible to meet, only to find extreme hostility from all involved when the truth came out—and it will come out. We don't work in a vacuum. Clients and sellers have moves to coordinate and may be involved in other closings. One small delay in one area has a domino effect that can wreak havoc in several people's lives. Even the smoothest closings and moves are stressful processes. Anything you can do to minimize your client's stress in the loan process will greatly reduce your stress and keep everyone happy! The earlier you address and resolve an issue, the less likely it will be to adversely impact the closing date.

Tip: When problems and issues arise, try to have a solution or alternative to present to the client. Work the issues as soon as they arise and keep the client (and realtors) informed throughout the process.

Successful originating and processing requires organization and attention to detail. I looked for these qualities above experience when hiring employees. Most people can be trained to become familiar with the programs and processes, but organization and attention to detail are character traits that come with the person. Our company had such a good reputation with our underwriters for providing complete, organized files that they would take ours ahead of other brokers' files into underwriting because they knew they could finish ours quickly. Another advantage to providing a complete and accurate file to the underwriter is goodwill. If the underwriter knows you set high standards for your files, they are more likely to work with you when issues arise.

Don't be afraid to make mistakes. There is no way you will ever know everything there is to know about every program, lender, or law. There is no way you will keep every client and realtor happy. Just use your best judgment and stay honest. If you are working with a good team of underwriters and attorneys, they won't let you get too far off track! If you do make a mistake, admit it, correct it, learn from it, and move on.

CHAPTER 2

General Information

Note: This chapter is an overview of the basic procedures used to originate and process a residential real estate mortgage application. Specific information and details are discussed in later chapters.

Whether you work for a mortgage broker or directly for a lender, the process is basically the same. The client completes the application and signs disclosures with a loan officer (loan origination). The file is given to the processor to collect and verify credit, income, and asset information needed for loan approval. The processor prepares the file for submission to the underwriter. Preparing the file for underwriting includes ordering reports (credit, appraisal, title commitments, and insurance declarations) and obtaining verifications (employment, asset, and rent or mortgage payments). The processor will obtain initial loan approval. Most lenders have an automated web site that allows electronic uploading and application approvals. If you work for a broker, you should identify the lender that has a program that is best suited to the client, using search criteria usually available on the lender's web site. Once the loan is submitted for approval, a credit report is usually ordered/obtained. If you switch lenders, you may have to re-run the credit report, although many systems will allow reports to be transferred from other lenders. Running multiple credit reports is costly (fees may be charged by each lender), and may adversely affect the client's credit score. For a client with low credit scores, multiple credit report runs could mean his scores will fall below approval guidelines and the loan will be declined.

The processor organizes the complete file, including income, asset, and liability documentation; employment and rent or mortgage verification(s); other documents, including a credit report, sales contract (for purchases), appraisal, insurance declarations, title commitment, and disclosures. Underwriters prefer information to be presented in a preset order to make it easier to find data and review the file for approval.

After processing, the completed file is submitted to the lender's underwriter who will approve the loan and authorize funding. Most lenders allow electronic submission of the file. The underwriter will issue a conditional approval: approved subject to submitting additional requested documentation known as conditions. Conditions will be anything that was not submitted in the original file that the underwriter requires for final approval and funding.

Once the underwriter clears the conditions on the file, you can order the closing package and funds for the loan.

Lenders fund loans from "warehouse lines of credit," a lender's credit line from a warehouse lender. The funded loans are usually sold to federally chartered shareholder-owned companies (Fannie Mae or Freddie Mac— see below) to reduce the amount of the lender's outstanding credit, thereby allowing the lender to fund more mortgage loans.

Fannie Mae and Freddie Mac have issued underwriting guidelines— criteria that mortgage application loan packages must meet to be eligible for purchase by the respective organization. Guidelines govern credit criteria, and allowable debt in relation to income, assets, and the property.

All lenders who sell loans to these organizations must abide by the same underwriting guidelines. Any loans that do not meet the guidelines will not be eligible for purchase by Fannie Mae and/or Freddie Mac and probably will be declined by the lender unless they have other programs available.

Fannie Mae is a shareholder-owned company with a federal charter to buy real estate mortgage loans from banks and lenders to maximize the availability of mortgage funds to homeowners. The mortgages back securities that are sold to investors. This practice allows banks and lenders to clear out their warehouse lines of credit so they have more money available to lend to other homeowners.

Freddie Mac is a similar program designed to help those with low and moderate incomes, including first-time home buyers, qualify for mortgage financing. Freddie Mac provides money for lenders to make mortgage loans readily available to the public.

Most of the lowest rate loans are underwritten, approved, and funded under Fannie Mae or Freddie Mac guidelines. Guidelines for individual programs change. For current guidelines on specific programs, check with your lenders.

Programs designed to help specific groups qualify for mortgage loans include Federal Housing Administration (FHA) and Veterans Administration guaranteed loans.

The Federal Housing Administration (FHA) provides mortgage insurance on FHA loans made by approved lenders, which minimizes lender risk. This allows lenders to provide mortgage loans to people who may not otherwise qualify for a loan. FHA programs require relatively low down payments and have flexible guidelines governing income requirements and debt ratios. The buyer pays private mortgage

5

insurance which allows the FHA to guarantee the loans made by the lenders.

The Veterans Administration (VA) guarantees mortgages requiring no down payment made by lenders to qualified veterans. The VA guarantees the loans made by approved lenders, allowing veterans access to favorable loan terms. The VA charges a funding fee, rather than private mortgage insurance, to the veteran home buyer which provides the funds for guaranteeing and buying back mortgage loans from the lenders in case of default by a veteran. The funding fee may be (and usually is) rolled into the loan amount, even if the loan to value exceeds 100 percent.

FHA and VA lenders must be approved by the respective organizations. Clients applying under these programs must be approved by the lender under the lender programs. FHA and VA do not approve or fund the loans; they guarantee the loans.

Subprime Mortgage Loans are loan programs for those with credit issues and lower credit scores, usually below 620 (see Chapter 11, Reviewing the Credit Report). Candidates for subprime mortgages cannot meet Fannie Mae or Freddie Mac guidelines and are ineligible for FHA and VA loans. Subprime mortgage rates are higher because the lender risk is higher. Subprime clients are those individuals who have had credit problems in the past including late payments, collections, judgments from creditors, and bankruptcies.

Given the recent shake-up of the mortgage industry, subprime mortgage programs are now harder to find. The requirements for approval are also more stringent. Many of the "A paper" (loan applications from clients with good credit) programs have also been affected. Lower or zero down payment programs are hard to find and have stricter approval criteria.

Private Mortgage Insurance

Private Mortgage Insurance (PMI) is insurance that protects lenders from foreclosure losses on low down payment loans for purchases or low equity on refinances (less than 20 percent). PMI helps minimize the risk a lender assumes in making a mortgage loan, allowing the lender to recover a portion of the investment should the client default on the loan and the property is foreclosed on. The amount of the premium is determined by the risk involved (no down payment? purchase? refinance? payment history?). To calculate current PMI factors and premium amounts, check the web site of PMI companies (www.mgic.com).

Beginning in 2007, PMI premiums may be tax deductible in some cases. Check the PMI (www.mgic.com) and IRS (www.irs.gov) web sites for the latest details.

Using a second mortgage may avoid the requirement for PMI. Generally, PMI is not required if the first mortgage is 80 percent or less of the purchase price (purchase) or appraised value (refinance). Discuss with the client the options and costs available to pay or avoid PMI, including adding a second mortgage to bring the first mortgage down to 80 percent.

Real Estate Settlement Procedures Act (RESPA)

RESPA is a federal statute first passed in 1974 to protect consumers in the purchase of residential real estate. The statute requires specific disclosures be given to the buyer and restricts certain practices by real estate professionals. Required disclosures include: settlement (closing) costs, loan servicing practices (the percentage of loans the lender sells), and business relationships, if any, among service providers (does the lender or broker have a financial interest in the credit report company, appraisal company, title company or other organization involved in the transaction?). **RESPA** prohibits the payment of referral fees or kickbacks by real estate professionals (mortgage brokers, loan officers, processors, and realtors, etc) involved in the transaction.

RESPA also says that the buyer chooses the closing attorney or title company used in the transaction. Many realtors and sellers think that if the seller pays closing costs, that the sellers get to choose. The logic behind the decision is that since the closing costs are coming out of the loan proceeds, the buyer is really paying and gets the choice of the closing attorney.

RESPA is a complicated statute; this book only gives you a very brief overview. Most mortgage broker and mortgage banker associations offer continuing education classes to help you understand and comply with **RESPA**. Be sure you take advantage of **RESPA** training that is available to you.

Watching for Fraud

With the technology available on desktop publishing today, it is relatively easy to generate income, asset, and employment documents. While most clients are honest, occasionally you may be given documents whose authenticity you question. Verify the documents' validity as much as you can. **Clients should never be given verifications to transport. You should always get the verifications yourself directly from the source.** Double-check business phone numbers from the phone book or Internet. Some small businesses operate with cell phones which may not be verifiable. Use your best judgment, and be as thorough as possible. If you think there is a problem, do not continue with the loan. You may be held responsible if you inadvertently submit fraudulent documents. Inform the client you cannot submit the documents to underwriting because they cannot be verified. You have a responsibility to the lender to submit verified documents to underwriting. You have a responsibility to yourself and your employer to maintain your integrity and high standards.

You also have a legal and moral responsibility to the client to find the best program for them and give them accurate information on programs and fees. Examples of fraud against the client for which you will be held responsible include: non-disclosure of fees, higher interest rates or fees at closing than promised, approving clients for programs with higher or adjusting rates they cannot afford, overstating income on stated income programs, and falsifying documents. **Fraudulent practices on the part of lenders and brokers have serious legal consequences.**

CHAPTER 3

Purchases vs. Refinances

Although processing requirements are similar for purchases and refinances, there are some fundamental differences to be considered. Purchases involve more people—buyers, sellers, and realtors. With more people involved, there are more issues, schedules, and priorities that must be considered. Purchases are usually on tighter schedules because both the buyers and sellers have moves to coordinate.

Purchases

A purchase involves transferring the title from one party to another. The lowest rate programs require a minimum of 5 percent of the sales price as a down payment. These loan amounts can be as high as 95 percent LTV (Loan-to-Value) which is the loan amount divided by the sales price. Purchases usually require the client to bring money to the closing. Funds for closing must come from an acceptable source (savings or tax refund, and **NOT** a cash advance on credit cards) as specified in the underwriting guidelines. Funds to close include the down payment, first year's homeowner's insurance premium, interest from the date of closing through the end of the month, and closing costs paid by the client, including the title insurance premium. The amount of money a client has available for closing will impact the program choice.

Closing costs cannot be rolled into the loan on purchases. The seller can pay closing costs from the proceeds of the loan.

Tip: Purchase contracts usually specify a closing date. Obtain the contract as soon as possible, even if not fully executed (signed by both buyer and seller). Once you have the contract and are reasonably sure both parties agree to the terms, get the title work and appraisal ordered (make sure you collect the appraisal money!) to have time to work out any issues that may come up prior to closing. If an inspection will be required, make sure the results are acceptable to the client before ordering the title work and appraisal.

(See Chapter 14, Ordering Appraisal, Title Work, and Insurance.)

Including the Spouse on the Loan and/or Deed

Many times two-income families will need the income from both spouses to qualify for the loan. If the clients' debt ratio is low and income from both spouses is not required for loan approval, both spouses are not required to be on the loan. If one spouse has credit problems, leaving him/her off the loan can result in loan approval on a lower rate, and better term loan program. Credit rating is an important consideration in the decision of whether or not to put a spouse on the loan. The loan will be graded/approved based upon the lowest middle credit score. If the spouse's income is not necessary for loan approval, the decision depends upon the credit rating and whether or not the spouse needs and/or wants the credit history of the mortgage on his/her credit report.

The spouse, or anyone else, can be on the deed without being on the loan. If the spouse, or anyone else, is on the loan, they MUST be on the deed.

If the spouse has court-ordered judgments on their credit report, which may result in liens being placed on the property after closing and recording the mortgage, the client may want to leave the spouse off the deed to avoid future issues. Clients with legal issues should discuss their situation with an attorney to determine the best way to proceed.

Co-Signers

Many clients ask about having a family member co-sign on the loan if the client has credit or debt ratio problems. Since the loan is graded/approved based upon the lowest credit score, a co-signer will not improve the package's credit grade or interest rate. Also, the co-signer must qualify based on his/her debt ratio including current rent or mortgage payment, the new mortgage payment in this transaction, as well as any debt showing on his/her credit report. This can be difficult for some co-signers. I rarely closed loans with co-signers. There are usually other programs that will work with the client only. I would usually work with the client to improve his financial and/or credit situation to be able to qualify on his own.

Dealing with Foreclosures

Purchasing foreclosures under market value can be a way to build equity quickly and is popular with investors. Financing foreclosures is more complicated than other purchases. Most foreclosures are sold "as is" which means the seller (usually the lender who now possesses the property) will not make any necessary repairs. Unfortunately, some former owners leave the property damaged. Foreclosures usually need repairs to meet Fannie Mae and Freddie Mac guidelines. All repairs indicated in the appraisal must be completed before the property will be accepted as collateral on Fannie Mae or Freddie Mac loan programs. If the property needs work, you will have to use a rehabilitation (rehab) loan, or construction type financing to purchase the property and get the deed in the client's name so work can begin. The rehab loan will lend an amount based upon the "subject to" value, or the value after repairs are made. Loan amounts and down payment requirements vary so check with several lenders. As a broker, I found that local banks are a good source for rehab money. Keep in mind these programs will require the client to have good credit. Rehab loan proceeds will be used to purchase the property (get the deed in the client's name) and complete the repairs. Once the repairs have been completed, the appraiser will re-inspect the property and the loan will be converted to permanent financing by the rehab lender or you can refinance them with another lender. Review the terms of available programs for permanent financing to determine the program and lender that is best for the client.

I had a client who found a great deal on a VA foreclosure that he intended to use as his primary residence. The property was to be sold "as is" and only needed about $500 of repairs to meet financing guidelines. The client was not able to get rehab financing due to his low credit scores. The client offered to pay for the repairs out of his pocket prior to closing but the VA refused to give him access to the property because of liability considerations. The lender stood firm on completing the repairs prior to closing and would not let the $500 be escrowed for repairs post closing. The client had to find another property and lost a good deal. *Clients who deal in foreclosures need cash and good credit!*

Another consideration with foreclosures is the former owner's right of redemption. Some states allow the previous owner an amount of time (usually one year) to redeem his property, called the redemption period. This right is rarely exercised because the previous owner must buy back the property and usually is not in a position to do so. Some lenders will fund purchases of foreclosures still in the redemption period if the title company will issue a redemption bond (the premium is included in the closing costs). Some lenders will not fund a foreclosure purchase at all until the property is out of the redemption period. If you are dealing with a foreclosure, check with your state and your lender to determine if there is a redemption period and what the lender requires.

Refinances

Rate/Term vs. Cash Out

A transaction is considered a refinance if at least one original title holder (owner of the property) remains on the deed. A rate/term refinance will pay off the existing loan and closing costs. A cash out refinance will pay off the existing mortgage plus closing costs and take equity out as cash or to pay off consumer debt. A transaction to pay a former spouse their share of equity in the subject property and remove them from the deed would be considered a cash out refinance.

Make sure the client is aware that **by federal law, refinances of primary residences (does not apply to investment property) have a three day right of rescission, which is the ability to cancel the transaction.** Funds will not be released until after midnight of the third day. The client can cancel the transaction during this three-day period. **According to RESPA, if the client cancels, all money paid by him must be refunded, even if you have already used it to pay for the credit report and appraisal.**

Weekdays and Saturdays are counted as rescission days. Funding days are business days only, no Saturdays. Sundays and holidays are never counted for either a rescission or a funding day.

There are some differences in the loan terms and underwriting requirements in rate/term and cash out refinances. Check with your lender's program guidelines for specific Loan-to-Value limits, interest rates, and maximum dollar amount of cash out. (**For refinances, Loan-to-Value equals loan amount divided by appraised value rather than the sales price for purchases.**) Using the appraised value of the property allows the client to take advantage of the equity in the property.

A rate/term refinance occurs when the client is paying off a first mortgage and rolling in the closing costs. Paying off a second mortgage can be considered rate/term IF it is a fixed rate second or a Home Equity Line of Credit (HELOC) that was used to purchase the home and *no additional draws have been made after closing*. If a HELOC is being paid through a rate/term refinance, an underwriter will usually require a copy of the settlement statement from the purchase to document that it originated during the original purchase transaction. On a rate/term refinance, the client can receive the lesser of $2,000 or 2 percent of the loan amount in cash at closing. If a client receives more cash than the lesser of $2,000 or 2 percent of the loan amount, the loan will be reclassified as a cash out and must be resubmitted to underwriting; possibly delaying the closing. **Be sure to be as accurate as possible when calculating the loan amount, closing costs, prepaids, and mortgage pay-offs. A final review before ordering the closing package should avoid this problem.** A cash out refinance allows the client to "cash out" equity in the property to pay off consumer debt or receive cash.

If the transaction is cash out, find out how much cash the client wants to receive at closing. When paying off consumer debt, the payoffs may be made by the attorney or title company at closing/funding and shown on the settlement statement, or the cash may be given directly to the client. If the debts are paid at closing, they are marked on the application as being paid at closing and not counted in the debt ratio. These debts must be paid by the attorney at closing to keep the debt ratio the same as the loan approval. Ask the client to give you copies of the latest statements on accounts to be paid off so you can submit them to the attorney. The sooner you do this the less likely closing/funding will be delayed because the attorney doesn't have payoff information. If the client will receive more than $20,000 cash out, the underwriter will require a letter of explanation (LOE) from the client stating what he intends to do with the cash. Some underwriters/programs require the LOE for lesser amounts. **The LOE should be general—payoff debt, home improvement, pay for college, etc., without going into a lot of detail, which may raise additional underwriting questions.**

Closing costs may be rolled into a refinance loan only. On a purchase, the sales price may be increased and the contract state that the seller is paying all or a portion of closing costs. Even though that sounds like rolling in closing costs, on a purchase, the seller is allowed to pay closing costs but the buyer is not allowed to roll them into the loan.

If a property has been listed for sale within the last twelve months, Fannie Mae/Freddie Mac guidelines will not allow refinance transactions.

CHAPTER 4

Getting Started

If the client submitted an Internet or e-mail application, take time to review it to see if the transaction is a purchase or refinance, the income and debt look to be within guidelines, and employment history looks stable. Based upon the type of transaction, identify the required documents and inform the client early enough to give him enough time to obtain them prior to the application interview. We had a standard document checklist for both purchases and refinances that we gave to clients (Exhibit 1) that listed required documentation. Once you have basic loan information, generate the initial Good Faith Estimate (GFE) and Truth-in-Lending (TIL) disclosures so you can discuss them in the interview. (See Chapter 7, Generating the GFE and TIL.) You will revise the GFE as you obtain specific information on closing costs and prepaids (homeowners' insurance premium and interest) but the initial disclosure will give the client an idea of what to expect at closing. I always tried to estimate high on the initial GFE, anticipating as many costs as possible given the client's situation. While most clients will accept some minor increases in closing cost estimates, rising closing costs will upset even the most patient client.

Organizing the File

With all the documents and disclosures involved in processing and closing a real estate loan application, as well as keeping up with the legal requirements to keep records, files must be organized and complete. The key is consistency with each file and each loan officer and processor. Consistency in organizing and documenting the files will also make it easier for others to quickly see the status of the file if they need to work on your file for you.

We developed an Information Sheet (Exhibit 2) which we clipped on the left inside cover of the file to capture the notes and contact information discussed in the next section. Completing the information sheet as you talk with your client will give you important information needed to effectively process the application package. Getting as much information as early as possible will help you avoid delays that could adversely affect the closing date.

We stapled a lined sheet of legal sized paper to the front cover of the file which we used as a status sheet. Any activity on the file, including phone calls with the client, was noted on the front, along with the date. This provides a quick and easy way to refresh your memory as well as let others who may work the file know what is going on. Keeping notes on who you talked to and when helps resolve issues. (Example: "Mr. Smith, according to my notes, when we spoke on the 18th you said you didn't want to lock your loan; you wanted to watch rates.") You have a lot more credibility when you keep a record of your work.

Our client files were legal size, with clips on both the right and left sides. The right side of the file contained all documents to be submitted to underwriting in the order we were submitting them. The left side of the file contained backup and supporting documents, including fax cover sheets used, e-mails, and invoices clipped behind the information sheet mentioned above. Organizing each file the same way helps ensure every file is complete and all lender and legal requirements are met. Another advantage is others can step in and work your file in your absence.

A red sticker on the tab of purchase files helps you to identify them faster. Purchases are usually on a stricter time schedule, with buyers and sellers scheduling movers, turning utilities on and off, etc. A delay on a purchase file can be extremely upsetting to all involved. Each day when you go through your files to see what needs to be done, a red sticker grabs your attention. The more files you are working, the more important identifying purchases quickly becomes.

Tip: Use a red sticker or other identifier to highlight purchase files.

Before the client Arrives

If the client completed an online application, print the application and generate a Good Faith Estimate (GFE) and Truth-In-Lending (TIL) form. **Both forms must be signed within three days of submission of the initial application,** *according to RESPA. If you can provide them at the initial application interview, you can save time. Make sure you disclose the required information during the initial interview. In addition, by providing the GFE and TIL during the initial application interview, you will be able to explain the forms and answer questions.*

(See Chapter 7 on preparing GFE and TIL.)

Documents the Client Should Bring to the Interview

When you set the appointment for the initial interview, make the client aware of the documentation required and have him bring as much as possible to the initial interview.

We created a document checklist for purchases and refinances to give to the client (Exhibit 1).

Purchases:

- Copy of the sales contract (if available)

- Full income documentation

  o Previous two years' W2s and latest pay stub

  o Award letters and bank statements showing deposits for social security and retirement income

  o For self-employed, or those relying on investment income to qualify. Collect two year's federal tax returns with all schedules.

- Asset documentation—statements covering sixty days on all accounts

- Copy of client's driver's license or other picture ID

- Names and contact numbers for the verbal VOE prior to closing

- Tell the client the fees for the credit report and appraisal

- Collect credit report fee and appraisal fee during the interview if applicable

Refinances:

- Full income documentation

  o Previous two years' W2s and latest pay stub

- o Award letters and bank statements showing deposits for social security and retirement income

- o For self-employed, or those relying on investment income to qualify, collect two years federal tax returns with all schedules

- Asset documentation, if the client will be bringing in funds to closing

- Copy of client's driver's license or other picture ID.

- Names and contact numbers for the verbal VOE prior to closing

- Tell the client the fees for the credit report and the appraisal

- Collect credit report and appraisal fee during the interview if applicable

- Copy of deed

- Copy of mortgage statement or payment coupon

- Copy of insurance declarations page

- Copy of title insurance policy, if available

- Copy of any credit card or loan statements to be paid by the refinance

Other Documentation, if applicable:

- Investment property leases

- Divorce decree (all pages)

- Bankruptcy papers (all pages)

- Gift letter

Tip: On refinances, collecting the deed, mortgage statement, and insurance declarations page will speed the processing time. Providing these documents to the attorney, title company, appraiser and client's insurance agent allow them to provide you with required documentation faster. The mortgage statement or payment coupon gives the attorney/title company the information required to order the payoff on the existing mortgage(s). If the client purchased owner's title insurance when they bought the home, the attorney/title company may be able to re-issue the existing policy rather than writing a new policy. Re-issuing the existing policy could save the client as much as 40 percent of the title insurance premium. Many times the client isn't sure if they have a title insurance policy or not. Have them check the settlement statement from the original purchase. Under the section for attorney fees, there will be a line for title insurance. If there is an amount by Owner's Premium, they have the insurance and should look in their files for the policy.

CHAPTER 5

Application Interview

The initial interview is much more than taking the application. It is an opportunity to get to know the clients, get an idea what their priorities are (lowest rate, minimum out-of-pocket costs), and identify any issues that could affect the program selection and loan approval. The initial interview is also an opportunity to explain the process, costs, and responsibilities to the client. Most people aren't very familiar with the mortgage loan process. Even those who are not first-time home buyers don't buy and sell real estate often enough to remember everything that goes on. Purchasing real estate involves a lot of money and legal procedures which can be very intimidating to clients. The initial interview is a great opportunity to explain the process and help them see they can trust you to guide them through. Once you have earned their trust, clients will be a great source of future business, referring friends and co-workers to you.

Collecting Required Information

The following information, which we collected on our Information Sheet, (Exhibit 2) should be obtained during the initial interview, along with completing the application and signing the disclosures.

Referred by: Always ask how the client heard of you/made the decision to use your company. This is very important for advertising and marketing decisions. If the client was referred by a realtor, former client, or others be sure to acknowledge and thank the person who recommended you. *Remember: referral fees and kickbacks are prohibited by RESPA!*

Date: the date the application was completed or downloaded from the Internet and signed by the client. This date triggers several disclosure requirements, including the Good Faith Estimate, Truth-in-Lending, and booklet on settlement procedures. If you can't give the client these disclosures when the application is submitted, you must send them within three days.

Type: Purchase or refinance; fixed rate or adjustable; Jumbo (loan amounts greater than $417,000 as of publication of this book). Try to get a general idea of what the client wants to do and identify potential issues.

Property Use and Type: The property use and type is crucial to the selection of the mortgage loan program. The property use will affect the down payment requirements and interest rates. Property use may also trigger some underwriting requirements. (Example: owning multiple investment properties requires the client to demonstrate two year's property management experience if he manages the properties himself.) Most programs have property restrictions, so always verify that the subject property will fit within the selected program guidelines.

Property Use:

- Primary residence—the client resides there at least 51 percent of the time

- Second home—vacation home; may not be rented to others

- Investment—produces rental income for the client

Property Type:

- Single family residence

- Condo

  o Low rise (equal to or less than four stories high)

  o High rise (more than four stories high)

  o Warrantable? (Considers such information as percent of complex complete vs. still under construction; percent of investors vs. primary residences in the complex)

- Townhouse

- Duplex

- Four-plex

- Apartment (commercial)

- Manufactured or modular home

- Log home

- Foreclosure?

Note: Many loan programs do not allow manufactured or log homes. Be sure to determine the type of property early in the processing period. The programs/lenders that do allow these unique properties require the appraiser to provide comparable sales of similar properties (log home or manufactured home sales) within a specified distance. This can be difficult or impossible which will cause the loan to be declined. Try to determine if the property is unique to the area as soon as possible. Many appraisers will let you know there may be a problem before he/she does the actual appraisal, avoiding the fee if the deal does not go through. Discuss possible issues with the appraiser BEFORE he does the work. Clients are understandably upset when they have paid for an appraisal that results in you telling them you can't close the loan!

Purchase or Refinance? If refinance, does the client want to roll closing costs into the loan? Does the client want cash out? *Remember, if the transaction involves a Home Equity Line of Credit (HELOC), you need to find out if the HELOC (pronounced "he-lock") was used to purchase the property and whether or not any additional draws have been made so you can determine if the refinance is a cash out or rate/term. If the HELOC was only used on the purchase with no additional draws, the client will need to provide you a copy of the settlement statement from the purchase closing.*

 Loan Amount: This can be an estimate, either a dollar amount or a description—payoff mortgage plus closing costs and prepaids (homeowner's insurance and interest) or a price range in a purchase. Jumbo loan programs (loan amounts greater than $417,000) have different requirements and rates from conforming programs. An initial estimate for the loan amount will allow you to start the approval process. The loan amount will be refined as you get more information about the transaction. On purchases, the loan amount will be the sales price less the down payment. The loan amount on refinances will be calculated based upon existing mortgage loan payoff(s), closing costs, and any cash out required.

Sales price: Either a price range the client is considering or an actual amount from the sales contract less the down payment.

Down payment: Dollar amount or percentage client will put down on a purchase. Discuss the documentation requirements for the down payment, including sourcing and seasoning (See Chapter 8, Selecting the Loan Program, section on Down Payment).

Term: Shown in months (360, 180, etc.). The term of the loan or repayment period will affect the interest rate. Generally, the shorter the term, the lower the interest rate.

Program: Thirty-year fixed, Adjustable rate, Jumbo, etc.

Special Issues: Find out if there is anything the client particularly wants/doesn't want or must have in the transaction (no Private Mortgage Insurance, a not-to-exceed loan amount, no escrows collected, must close by a certain date, etc.). Any credit or legal issues should be identified as soon as possible to determine if they can be resolved or a program can be found to accommodate them. **Explain the importance of no major changes in credit, debt, or income once loan approval is obtained. If there is a change in circumstances, the client should notify you immediately so you can determine the impact on the approval.**

Realtors: On purchases, find out if there are realtors involved. If so, get the names and contact numbers of the listing agent (represents seller) and the selling agent (represents buyer). It is important to keep in contact with everyone involved in the transaction to let them know the status/progress. To save time and numerous phone calls, ask the selling agent to be the main point of contact and disseminate the information to the listing agent and seller.

Attorney/Title Company: Remember, RESPA says the choice of attorney/title company is the buyer's, even if the sellers are paying the closing costs. Technically, the buyer is paying the closing costs because it is part of the purchase price. Many realtors will tell you if the seller is paying the closing costs, the seller gets to choose the attorney. This is not true; however, if the buyer doesn't have a preference, using the seller's choice will avoid conflict. If the buyer prefers using a specific attorney/title company, you must use the buyer's choice. Note the preference on the file.

Insurance: On purchases, the first year's homeowner's insurance premium must be paid at closing. On refinances, the amount of the insurance premium collected at closing will depend upon the premium due date (if the client is not changing insurance carriers). Get the contact information for the homeowner's insurance agent. On purchases, the client may not have decided. Let him know he needs to start looking for the one he wants to use, and then he must let you know as soon as possible. **Most programs will not allow a deductible to exceed $1,000.** Most lenders won't let you order the closing package without prior submission of the declarations page to underwriting.

Credit report: Collect the credit report fee during the application interview. Make a note on the file of the date and amount paid. The credit report fee will be shown as a POC (Paid Outside of Closing) cost on the settlement statement. **If there will be a co-borrower who is not the spouse of the client, two credit reports must be run. Only married co-borrowers' credit may be run together.**

Appraisal: If the client has a preference for the appraiser, note it on the file. (They usually don't.) Otherwise, you can use your appraisers. I collected the fee prior to ordering the appraisal since I was liable for the fee regardless of whether the client changed lenders, or changed their minds, etc. On a purchase, I recommend the appraisal not be ordered (it can be paid for any time) prior to the inspection, if one is to be done, and after loan approval. Usually there are no problems large enough to cancel the contract but sometimes the client will cancel based upon the results of the inspection. Once the appraisal has been ordered and completed, you will owe the fee, even if the contract is cancelled. On a refinance, the appraisal can be ordered after loan approval. Make sure all appraiser contact information is noted on the file. Also make sure the appraiser is approved by the lender. Note the date and amount paid on the file.

Additional Charges: Keep a record of additional fees/charges to be collected at closing. These could include additional appraisal charges for extra comparables, schedules, etc., and fees charged by banks for verifications or subordination agreements. **If you incur additional fees as you process the loan, BE SURE to discuss the fees, as well as the necessity for them, with your client before the fees are incurred! Remember to add the fees to the Good Faith Estimate (GFE).** Submit copies of invoices to the closing attorney for all third-party fees to be collected at closing. Be sure to list these fees when ordering the closing package to ensure the fees will be on the settlement statement and collected at closing or shown as a Paid Outside Closing fee. Most lenders will charge a fee to re-draw the closing package to add additional fees.

FHA payoff?

If the transaction is paying off an FHA loan, the FHA lender must receive the payoff funds by the first day of the month at 1:00 p.m. lender's time. Closing should be planned accordingly and all parties involved should be notified.

Existing second? (refinances only)

If a second mortgage exists, determine if the client wants to pay it off in this transaction. *Remember,* if the second is a HELOC, the transaction **may** be treated as a cash out (see the section on Refinances, above).

Cheryl L. Peck

Determine the amount of the existing second, since the amount will affect the Total Loan-To-Value (LTV) and may affect the program. If the second mortgage is a HELOC and is to be left open, **the amount considered in the LTV is the HELOC ceiling, not the current principal balance.** If a second is to be left open rather than paid off, the lender will require a subordination agreement to allow the current second to remain in second place after the refinance. **Some second mortgage lenders charge a fee to generate the subordination agreement. If so, be sure to collect it from the client or have the client order the subordination agreement directly from the second mortgage lender.**

Escrows collected?

Most mortgage loan servicers will set up an account, an escrow account, to collect monthly property tax and homeowner's insurance premium payments. The property tax bill and annual homeowner's insurance premium are divided by twelve and added to the loan's principal and interest payment. Each year when the property taxes and homeowner's insurance premium are due, the mortgage company pays them from the money in the escrow account. Collecting money for the escrow account each month is usually optional. Determine if the client wants the taxes and insurance collected as part of the payment each month and paid by the lender when due. Most lenders require a hit to the points—not the rate (usually 25 percent) if the client does not escrow. Explain to the client how the amounts of taxes and insurance are determined and whether or not this can be included in the loan. The amount of money collected at closing to start the escrow account, along with interest collected from the date of funding through the end of the month, are called prepaids (prepaid closing costs). Prepaids may be rolled into the loan on a refinance but not a purchase. See section e., Estimate Prepaid Items under Details of Transaction, page 4 of the application.

For first-time home buyers or subprime clients, I usually did not offer the option not to collect escrows. There are many examples where new homeowners lose or almost lose their home because they didn't have escrows collected by the lender and didn't have the money to pay the taxes and insurance when due.

CHAPTER 6

Taking the Application

The application form is referred to by number—1003 (ten-o-three). Those new to the industry usually call it a "one thousand three" and usually get a laugh from those who have been in the business longer. The only reason I can think of for referring to it as a ten-o-three rather than a one-thousand-three is fewer syllables. I guess mortgage professionals are in a hurry.

The Application

Page 1

Complete each section as completely as possible.

I. Type of mortgage and terms of loan. Type: (VA, FHA, USDA Rural Housing) Loan Amount, Interest Rate, Number of Months, Fixed or Adjustable Rate.

II. Property Information and Purpose of Loan. Subject property address, number of units, year built, legal description (if unknown put "See Title"), purpose, and property use.

If construction/perm, list year lot acquired, original cost, amount of existing liens, present value of lot, and cost of improvements.

<u>Title</u>: List the names to be on the deed/title and vesting (unmarried man, husband and wife, etc.). On a refinance, the names on the title generally do not change (unless a divorce is involved). On purchases, be sure you ask how the name(s) should be listed on the title. Be aware that if a married person is listed alone on the title for the primary residence, the spouse may be required to sign some of the closing documents (mortgage, truth-in-lending, etc.). A person can be on the deed without being on the loan/note. The reverse is not true. If a person is on the loan/note, they must be on the deed.

If the transaction is a refinance, enter the appropriate information. The amount of the existing loan(s) can be added once you obtain the credit report.

III. Borrower Information. Complete this section as thoroughly as possible. Some information, such as name, social security number, and birth date, are required. Provide two years' address of primary residence information. **The address must be a street address and not a post office box.** The post office box can be listed as a mailing address. *If the client rents, ask if they rent from a property management company or if they pay an individual by check.* Some programs require twelve months' cancelled rent checks if the landlord is an individual. **Cash rent payments to an individual landlord cannot be documented.** An underwriter will not accept receipts from an individual landlord to document cash rent payments. If a property management company collects the rent, cash payments are acceptable. The property management company will complete a Verification of Rent. The ability to document rent payments may affect the choice of loan program.

Page 2

<u>**IV. Employment Information.**</u> Include employer's address and phone number covering a two-year period. Frequent job changes over a two-year period indicates job instability and raises a red flag to an underwriter, who may look closer at the file before issuing an approval. For current employment, I got the name and phone number of several co-workers who can verify employment. Most lenders require their closing department employees to call for a verbal verification of employment (VOE) before the closing package is released. If the closer cannot contact anyone, the closing may be delayed. Usually, the closer will only ask if the client is still employed so the contact doesn't have to know hire dates, salary, etc. I make a note on the initial 1003 listing contact information for the verbal VOE. Explain the verbal VOE requirement to the client so they can make co-workers aware of the call. I also provided the underwriter with two or three contacts for the verbal VOE so that the release of the closing package would not be delayed if a contact could not be reached. I had several clients through the years who quit their job or were laid off between application and closing. This can be extremely unpleasant on a purchase transaction! If you explain to the client that the underwriter will verify that they are still working before the release of the closing package, they will usually avoid surprising everyone before closing, by having no job.

Tip: Getting several contacts from the client for the pre-closing verbal VOE early may avoid delays in issuing the closing package and help the client understand the importance of no employment changes prior to closing.

<u>**V. Monthly Income and Combined Housing Expense Information.**</u>

<u>Gross Monthly Income.</u> Input the base income based on the W2s and pay stub showing year-to-date income provided. To calculate base income:

1. Hourly rate * number of hours per pay period * number of pay periods per year / 12 = gross monthly income

   (Example: $24 per hour, paid bi-weekly: 24 * 80 = $1,920 * 26 = $49,920 annual / 12 = $4,160 per month.) Note: DO NOT use four weeks per month, since you will understate income.

2. Annual divided by 12 = gross monthly income

Overtime, bonuses, and commission, rental income, dividend and interest income may be used only if the client has been receiving it for two years (documented by federal tax returns) or Verification of Employment (VOE) and the extra income is likely to continue. If the overtime or commission income is not the same each month, average the last twenty-four months to use for approval.

Retirement/social security income is listed under "Other" income. Documentation must show the client is: 1) Entitled to receive the income (award letter), and 2) Actually receives the income (most have the money direct deposited into their bank accounts, so two months' statements showing the deposits are usually enough documentation to count the income).

Alimony or child support income is documented by providing the complete divorce decree. The age or birth dates of the children should be listed, otherwise the client will have to provide birth certificates or other documentation of the children's ages. To use alimony or child support income, the income must continue for three years from loan closing. Some loan programs, especially subprime programs, require documentation that the client is actually receiving the alimony or child support payments. Sometimes this is difficult or impossible to provide if the transaction does not involve an outside agency (court administered or payroll deducted by employer). If the exact amount is not deposited each time in the bank account, payments cannot be documented by bank statements. Providing cancelled checks (front and back) will document the payments, if the former spouse is willing to provide them.

Self-employment income is documented with two years' federal tax returns, including all schedules. Calculating self-employment income can be complex. Take advantage of available training.

A person operating a sole proprietorship will show business income and deductions with a 1040 Schedule C Profit or Loss from Business. Net profit (or loss) (line 31) for the last two years divided by twenty-four is used for monthly income for loan approval. Financial statements from a Certified Public Accountant (CPA) will document year-to-date income for the current year. If the client has depreciation listed on the Schedule C, the amount of the depreciation should be added to the net income since depreciation is not a cash expense. If Schedule C does not show enough income for loan approval and there is no other income to be counted, you must consider a stated income program.

Real estate investment income is shown on 1040 Schedule E, Supplemental Income and Loss. Income, or loss, is shown on line 26, Total rental real estate or royalty income (or loss). Divide by twelve for monthly income/loss.

Self-employed clients who have ownership of a corporation or partnership will report their share of profits, based on their percentage of ownership, on Schedule K-1.

Self-employed clients with an ownership interest in a corporation or Limited Liability Company (LLC) (also reports individual shares of company profits on a Schedule K Form 1065) may have W2 income from the company. You can count the W2 income if they have been receiving it for at least two years. You will need the standard income documentation of W2s and latest pay stub. You will also need the tax returns with the Schedule Ks included because the client is still considered self-employed if they have at least a 25 percent ownership interest in the company.

When tax returns are provided to document income, the client(s) must sign both the 1040 form and a 4506-T, which allows the lender to order the tax returns from the Internal Revenue Service (IRS). **Be aware that many lenders require the underwriter to automatically order the return from the IRS and compare it to the forms submitted by the client in the loan application package.** A discrepancy in the two forms is considered client fraud. I would always explain the purpose of the 4506-T and tell the client that the underwriter would compare what they submitted to me with what they submitted to the IRS.

Most self-employed clients must use stated income programs because they cannot document income. (**Note:** Stated income programs are designed for clients who cannot document income in the traditional ways. **IT IS NOT** designed as an opportunity to make up income that doesn't exist!) If you use a stated income program, make sure your client has sufficient income to meet debt ratio requirements. It is unethical, irresponsible, and illegal to overstate income just to get the loan approved. Some subprime programs will use twelve to twenty-four months of bank statements and average the deposits to determine self-employment income, but rates are usually significantly higher. If you are using **stated income programs**, be sure **NOT to include ANY income documentation!** Examine bank statements and other assets to insure no income information is included. Sometimes the client will have other income, such as social security or retirement that is deposited directly into his bank account. When using these statements to document assets, use a black marker to mark out the amount. If you are using IRS form Schedule C to document two years' self-employment history, mark out all figures. *Failure to do so may result in the loan being declined.*

<u>Net Rental Income</u>: Net rental income (you can only count 75 percent of monthly rent; 25 percent is considered set aside for repairs and maintenance) will be calculated from information added under Schedule of Real Estate Owned on page 3 of the 1003. If 75 percent of the rent is more than the mortgage payment, including taxes and insurance, of the rental property, net rent will be positive and counted as income. If the mortgage payment, taxes and insurance is more than 75 percent of the rent, net rent will be negative. The negative amount will be counted in the debt ratio.

Tip: If the client had only one or two investment properties and had enough documented income to cover all his debt, including investment property mortgage payments, taxes, and insurance; I didn't count rental income and avoided some paperwork!

If a client has multiple investment properties, you will usually have to document rental income to qualify for your transaction approval. Rental income documentation includes a lease and the latest two years of IRS Schedule E. If you use a stated income program, no rental income documentation is required. You should include two years' IRS Schedule E forms to document two years of property management experience. **BE SURE TO MARK OUT DOLLAR AMOUNTS ON THE FORMS FOR STATED INCOME PROGRAMS! Stated income programs do not allow ANY income documentation or the loan could be declined.**

Note: If the client has multiple rental properties and you are using rental income for loan approval, a minimum of two years' property management experience is required. (Submitting two years of Schedule E from the tax returns will qualify.) If the client uses a professional property management company (not his own) the two years experience requirement is waived.

<u>Monthly Housing Expenses</u>: List existing rent or mortgage payments, including second mortgage, if any. If the mortgage payment includes taxes and insurance, note "included" on the lines for taxes and insurance. For proposed housing expenses, the application software should calculate principal and interest payments based upon the loan information provided. Taxes and insurance should be added when determined. If there are monthly homeowner's association dues, be sure to add those because they will affect the debt ratio. If the loan amount is more than 80 percent of the appraised value (refinances) or sales price (purchases) Private Mortgage Insurance (PMI) will apply. Private mortgage insurance rates may be calculated from www.mgic.com. **Try to obtain correct tax and insurance information as soon as possible, add the data to the 1003 and re-run the approval (see section on Approvals). Some debt ratios are so close to approval ceilings, that taxes and/or insurance may affect the approval.**

Page 3

VI. Assets and Liabilities.

<u>Assets</u>: On purchases, assets must be documented showing funds to close. Documentation should cover sixty days. Any large deposits must be documented and explained. I always advised clients to start building savings as soon as possible once they decided to buy a house to make sure they had the required funds and to make sure they were "seasoned" (at least sixty days old). For refinances, if the client is financing the total outstanding mortgage balance and rolling closing into the loan, no assets are required. I usually listed $1.00 under assets (some lender approval systems require an asset balance greater than zero). There is no documentation required. If the client is paying down the mortgage balance or bringing in closing, documentation of funds to close is required.

Tip: For rate/term refinances where the client will not be bringing any money to closing, (with closing costs rolled into the loan) listing the asset amount as $1.00 eliminates the necessity to obtain asset documentation.

Fannie Mae and Freddie Mac underwriting guidelines also have requirements/restrictions on the source of funds to close. If the money has been in the client's account for sixty days, it is automatically sourced and seasoned. (Sourced: where the money came from; Seasoned: how long the money has been in the client's bank account.) If not, you must document where/how the client obtained the funds to close. Some programs allow a gift from a relative (immediate family). Other acceptable sources include selling an asset, advances on salary and/or commission, tax refunds, or equity in existing property. Check the guidelines on the specific program to determine acceptable sources of assets. Documenting the source of funds to close can be difficult, if not impossible. I had a client who sold a motorcycle for the down payment on his house. The underwriter required not only the bill of sale (which could easily be produced) but also the registration of the bike in the new owner's name. Fortunately, the buyer was a friend of the client so it was easy to get. If the source of funds is other than savings or a gift, be sure to check with the underwriter to determine what documentation is required.

The amount of money the client has available for down payment and closing costs will affect the program options available to the client. The lowest rate programs require a minimum of 5 percent down. It is extremely important to discuss funds required for closing during the initial interview to determine how much is available and *where it is coming from.* Sometimes the client is vague about the source and amount. Try to get specific information so you can advise them on programs available to them as well as acceptable sources of funds to close. Some programs allow gift funds; some require the client's own funds seasoned for sixty days. If the client is just beginning the search for a home, they should have time to build some assets for closing. I would tell clients to start putting as much money as possible into one account as soon as possible and to avoid any unnecessary expenses. If a major expense comes up unexpectedly, the client should call you to discuss the impact on the loan application.

Most programs limit the amount of funds a seller can contribute to closing. Called seller concessions, closing costs are usually described as a percentage of the sales price. The lowest rate, 95 percent programs **allow seller concessions up to 3 percent of the sales price for primary residences and 2 percent for investment property. Many times buyers, sellers, and realtors are not aware of the lower amount sellers are allowed to contribute to closing costs on the purchase of investment property.** *Make sure everyone, including the seller, is aware of any program restrictions on seller concessions early in the process.* They may want to revise the contract given the program restrictions. Both the client and the seller (and the real estate agents) can get extremely upset if you tell them late in the process that the program won't allow the amount of seller concessions specified in the contract.

Liabilities: The client should list all debt on the initial application. The liabilities on the initial 1003 is rarely accurate or complete. For loan approval, the liability section should match the credit report. Any liability that appears on the credit report but not on the initial application should be discussed with the client. If the debt has been paid, the client should be able to provide documentation. After the application is run through the lender's approval system and a credit report is available, correct the liabilities section to match the credit report. The liabilities section should include the creditor name and account number, type of debt (mortgage, installment, revolving), current balance, and payment amount. Debt that will be paid within ten months, according to the credit report (ten payments are greater than or equal to the balance), do not have to be counted. Any debt that will be paid off with this transaction (cash out refinance) should be noted by checking the "will be paid" box. Stress to the client that any new debt incurred before the closing/funding of this loan may result in denial of this loan. The client should avoid any new debt. If circumstances require new debt (need a new car to get to work), they should call you first to determine the impact on their loan approval. Ideally, the client should wait until after closing to incur new debt. If unavoidable, you will have to reassess the loan given the additional debt. After the liabilities on the 1003 have been edited to match the credit report, re-run the approval with the correct debt.

Mortgage Liabilities: An "M" in the type of debt box will indicate a mortgage liability. Usually the payment will be in parenthesis which means it will not be counted in the debt ratio. If the debt is not being paid by this transaction, it should be counted in the debt ratio, so I usually marked the debt as an "L" for installment loan. If the mortgage liability was on investment property and we were not counting rental income, I marked the debt as "L" so the liability would count on the debt ratio. If rental income and liability are counted under net rent, the debt can be marked as "M."

Verifying rent or mortgage payments not shown on the credit report: If the client rents from a property management company, a completed Verification of Rent form is usually enough to document on-time rent payments. If renting from an individual, twelve months' cancelled checks may required. Most landlords prefer cash so it may not be possible to document rent. This is important to discover during the initial interview because it can affect the choice of loan program. Some programs do not require rent to be verified, especially if the client's credit score is high (680 or above).

Other Liabilities: Alimony and child support paid are liabilities documented by the *entire* divorce decree.

<u>Schedule of Real Estate Owned</u>: Enter the subject property information first if the transaction is a refinance. List the primary residence ahead of investment property. On purchase transactions of primary residences, if the client has a current primary residence to sell, **DO NOT** put PS (Pending Sale) in the disposition box **unless** the house will be sold prior to closing this transaction. A "PS" will require a settlement statement showing the property was sold and the mortgage has been paid off prior to closing this transaction. Just because the house is on the market does not make it a pending sale! Note: if the current primary residence will not be sold before closing this transaction, the mortgage payment must be considered in the debt ratio. If the current residence will be sold prior to closing this transaction, mark PS and do not count the current mortgage payments in the debt ratio. The underwriter will require a copy of the settlement statement prior to clearing the file for closing to document the sale and the availability of funds for down payment and closing costs in this transaction. The settlement statement is considered valid documentation of sourced and seasoned funds. Because the sale of the current residence is often within a day, or even the same day, as closing this transaction, the underwriter will make the settlement statement on the sale of the current residence a Prior-to-Funding condition, allowing you to order the closing package. Your work is simplified if the same attorney is closing both transactions. Otherwise you must make sure you obtain the first settlement statement and get it to the underwriter and closing department.

<u>Multiple Mortgaged Properties</u>: Properties listed in the Schedule of Real Estate Owned section should be matched with the mortgage liabilities on the credit report and the liabilities section of the application. To make it easier for the underwriter and the processors, I would cross-reference the properties and mortgages by putting the address of the property under the creditor's name in the liability section. Also, I would list the creditor's

name by the property in the Remarks section of Real Estate Owned. Be sure to look for any second mortgages. With multiple properties you should ask the client which mortgages are for which properties. **You should ask the client for copies of mortgage statements on any mortgaged property that is not being paid by this transaction. The underwriter will want to make sure the total payment includes taxes and insurance. Otherwise you will have to document and count the taxes and insurance as additional debt.**

Tip: Match addresses with liabilities for multiple mortgaged properties on both the liability and real estate owned sections of the 1003 to make sure the 1003 is accurate and complete which will simplify underwriting.

Non-mortgaged properties: For real estate that has no liens (mortgages), an underwriter will require documentation that property owned with no creditor on the credit report is not financed privately. If the property has a structure on it, an insurance declarations page showing a no mortgage clause will usually suffice. A vacant lot requiring no insurance is harder to document. An underwriter may take property tax documentation (unimproved property taxes are obviously lower than improved property). If proper documentation is not provided, an underwriter may require a title search on the property which is costly and time consuming. This also irritates the client.

Page 4

VII. Details of Transaction.

The details of transaction section will usually be blank on the initial 1003. Your application system will generate data for the final 1003. The data should be as accurate as possible. Many underwriters use the total on the Cash from/to Borrower line to determine how much money should be documented for closing. (Cash from Borrower means the client must bring money to the closing. Cash to Borrower means the client will receive money at the closing.) If you go too high on this line, the client may not be able to document enough assets; too low and the client may have a problem coming up with the money to close. Try to figure the amount of money the client must bring to closing as closely as possible, estimating high. Let the client know early in the process so they can make sure they have enough money. Canceling a closing because the client can't come up with the money is not a pleasant experience, especially if you never told them how much they could expect to bring in.

a. Purchase Price—Total sales price taken from the sales contract. If the client is getting pre-approved prior to making an offer on a house, put the high end of the price range the client is considering.

b. Alterations—Estimated cost of improvements (for new construction or home improvement loans). This box will not be used for most purchases.

c. Land—Cost of the lot (construction or lot loans).

d. Refinance—The total amount of debt to be refinanced, including first and second mortgages and other consumer debt. If you have checked the "Will be paid off" box in the Liability section, the total will be calculated for you automatically.

Tip: When paying off an existing first mortgage on refinances, I always added a payment to the balance on the credit report to be sure to include any accrued interest and other fees so that the total payoff amount is accurately reflected here. You can also add the correct payoff amount once the current lender provides it. Otherwise, the loan amount will not be high enough to pay off everything and the client will have to bring money to closing. This is generally a bad thing to tell the client right before closing.

e. <u>Estimated prepaid items</u>—If you have entered these amounts in the Good Faith Estimate, most processing software systems will automatically include the amount here. Prepaid items consist of interest from date of funding through the end of the month and homeowner's insurance premiums. On purchases, the first year's homeowner's insurance premium is collected at closing. I also add three month's insurance premiums and three month's property taxes to the escrow account for the cushion. On refinances, check the current insurance declarations page to determine the policy premium due date. Count the number of mortgage payments collected between the funding date and the homeowner's premium due date. Collect the difference of the premium amount less the amount collected in payments prior to the due date, plus the three month's cushion. This amount will usually be a high enough estimate to ensure the client does not have to bring money to closing.

f. <u>Estimated closing costs</u>—Your application software should automatically complete this line from the Good Faith Estimate. Review the Good Faith Estimate for accuracy. Be sure to add additional fees that have accrued during the process.

g. <u>PMI, MIP, Funding Fee</u>—Private mortgage insurance rates may be estimated using the web site www.mgic.com. Funding fees, which eliminate PMI requirements, are required on VA loans. Check with the VA for current factors for the funding fees.

h. <u>Discount (if borrower will pay)</u>—The amount of any points charged to buy the rate down.

i. <u>Total Costs</u>—This field is automatically calculated.

j. <u>Subordinate Financing</u>—List the amount of an existing or new second mortgage here. If this package is for a second mortgage, list the amount of the existing or new first mortgage here.

This allows accurate LTV/CLTV amounts to be listed on the Transmittal Summary (Form 1008, pronounced ten-o-eight).

k. <u>Closing Costs Paid By Seller</u>—For purchases. (Obviously!) Check the contract for the amount, if any, that the seller is willing to pay. Make sure the amount is allowable under the specific mortgage program your client is using.

l. <u>Additional Credits</u>—Any money paid by the client outside of closing should be listed here. This can include earnest money, appraisal and credit report fees.

m. <u>Loan Amount</u>—The amount of the loan in this transaction. It is automatically entered here.

n. <u>PMI, MIP financed</u>—The amount, if any, that is included in the loan.

o. <u>Loan Amount</u>—(m + n)

p. <u>Cash from/to borrower</u>—Most loan programs will not allow a borrower to receive cash at closing from the seller on a purchase. If the program was a no down payment program, the client paid earnest money, and the seller paid all the closing costs, it is possible for the borrower to receive money back that they paid outside of closing. The client may receive any excess money he paid back at closing. An accurate estimate of all fees will give you an idea if the client should expect to receive any money back. On a rate/term refinance, the client can receive up to 2 percent of the loan amount or $2,000, whichever is less at funding. On a cash out refinance, the amount of cash the client can receive will be stated in the program requirements. An accurate Good Faith Estimate, including taxes and insurance information, will ensure an accurate amount the client should expect to bring to closing. I always tried to estimate high so the client was sure to have enough money. Also, it's easier to tell the client he must bring in less money than you told him than if you have to tell him he must bring in more. Underestimating the amount of money to bring to closing can ruin the deal. Some clients barely have enough to close the transaction. Any underestimated costs or unexpected fees can result in the client not having enough money, or enough sourced and seasoned money. An underwriter will review this line against the assets you have submitted to determine the amount of assets they require to be documented. Overestimating the funds to close may cause a problem in documenting assets. Underestimating funds to close may put the client in a bind right before closing.

VIII. Declarations.

Have the client(s) answer questions a. through m. as thoroughly as possible. A "yes" answer for questions a. through g. require an explanation on page 5. Review the client's answers to make sure they are correct. For some reason, a frequent mistake is marking "yes" to both "Are you a permanent resident alien?" and "Are you a U.S. citizen?" Once, a young first-time home buyer marked yes to the question, "Have you had an ownership interest in a property in the last three years?" I reminded him he had never owned a home before. He said no, but he had an interest in owning a home!

If the client is not a U.S. citizen, get a copy (front and back) of his "green card" or visa. There are many different types of visas. Each loan program will specify which visas are required for a non-citizen to purchase property in the United States.

If the subject property is a second home, marking "No" for question l, "Do you intend to occupy the property as your primary residence?" may cause a glitch in the lender's automated underwriting system because it may classify the property as investment. If the LTV is

higher than the investment property programs allow, you won't get an approval. Since you have all the information entered correctly, it takes forever to discover the problem. Check with your underwriter to see how to handle it. I was usually told to check "yes" in the lender's approval system (not the client's 1003), and then let the underwriter know that the package should be reviewed as a second home.

IX. Information for Government Monitoring Purposes.

If the client checks the box next to, "I do not wish to furnish this information," the loan officer who takes the application must complete Section IX. If the application is taken by phone or through the Internet, the loan officer should try to determine the correct responses based upon a conversation with the client(s).

Make sure the method used to take the application is noted. The interviewer should complete their contact information.

The original application should be signed and dated by the client(s). Remember that the date the application is submitted and signed triggers the RESPA disclosures, GFE, and TIL, which must be presented to the client within three days of the application date.

If the transaction is a purchase and the client is currently renting, remind him to check into changing his withholding exemptions. Since he will now be able to deduct mortgage interest and property taxes from his taxable income, his tax bill will be lower. No changes to withholding will make the refund significantly larger. Have him check with his personnel or human resources department for more information. Or he can go online to www.irs.gov and look at the Employers' Guide to Withholding. This booklet has tables defining the dollar amount of one exemption, given: 1) the amount he gets paid; 2) the frequency he gets paid; and 3) filing status (single, married filing jointly, etc.).

Before the client leaves the interview, make sure you have checked each of the items as noted below.

- Each page of the application package has been signed and dated, including all disclosures.

- The client has received copies of all required disclosures and notices.

- Make sure you have a copy of all required documentation, or have arranged with the client to bring it in.

- You have contact numbers for the client. Ask if it is okay to call him at work.

- You have contact numbers for the verbal verification of employment (done by the underwriter prior to releasing the closing package). **Without the verbal verification, the closing package will not go out and you can't close!** The verification ensures the borrower is still on the job; details about dates and salary amount are not necessary. Try to get more than one contact name and number so that the underwriter is likely to reach someone and not delay the release of the closing package.

- The client knows to contact you if there are any changes in employment, income, debt, or credit rating as soon as possible. Given enough notice, you can usually work around most issues. Finding out the day before closing that the client spent the funds to close on a car will stop the closing. I have had clients quit their job the day before closing and had clients who filed bankruptcy during the processing period. In most of those cases, the client was upset with me because I had originally told them they were approved!

- Collect any fees Paid Outside of Closing (POC), such as a credit report or appraisal money, if applicable.

CHAPTER 7

Generating the Good Faith Estimate (GFE), the Truth-In-Lending (TIL) and Other Disclosures

RESPA requires that the Good Faith Estimate and the Truth-In-Lending disclosures, along with a booklet explaining closing costs, are required to be given to the client within three days of the date of the original application (1003). If the application is a mail-out, you must send the disclosures out within the three days. The client should sign, date, and return the disclosures to you. If they do not, put a copy in the file with a note on the disclosure stating when the disclosures were sent and that they were not returned by the client. If the client is coming into the office, provide the disclosures for signature then. Sometimes it is difficult to accurately reflect costs this early in the process. Once the credit report is reviewed, it may be necessary to change programs or lenders. However, make the initial disclosures as accurate and complete as possible. You will revise and reissue the disclosures as you receive additional information during the process. If the final costs are higher than the initial disclosures, be sure you re-disclose these amounts to your client. You do **NOT** want the client to discover at closing that the closing costs and interest rates were higher than you said. Some states require re-disclosure to the client if the GFE increases by a certain percentage, usually 3 percent or more. If this applies to your transaction, be sure to get an updated GFE signed by the client, and put it in your file.

Good Faith Estimate

If you use multiple lenders, your application software should allow you to input fees for several lenders. If you work for a lender you also should have the fees input into your application software. Having the data pre-loaded will save you a lot of time generating the disclosures. Make sure any recent changes in fees are reflected in your database. **Lender fees** which have "PFC" (Prepaid Finance Charge) checked will be reflected in the Annual Percentage Rate. If you aren't sure which charges apply, especially since different lenders may use different terms for essentially the same fee, review the settlement statements of closed files or talk to the lender's closing department.

As you prepare an individual GFE, review the file to make sure you include any required fees that are not generally included. For instance, some second mortgage lenders charge a fee to subordinate the loan. If you are refinancing a first with an existing second, you may incur a subordination fee from the second mortgage lender as much as $100.00 or more. You probably won't have all the information when you provide the initial disclosures. As soon as you discover an additional fee, be sure to include it in your GFE so that you will have an accurate estimate of closing costs to provide to the client.

Prepaids, or items required to be paid in advance, include interest, homeowner's insurance, mortgage insurance, and funding fees. During the initial interview, you probably will not have enough information to provide accurate amounts of these items. As you process the loan and determine an interest rate, closing date, and loan program, you can refine the GFE.

Prepaid interest is collected from the date of funding through the end of the calendar month. A purchase transaction funds the date of closing. A refinance of a primary residence or second home funds after the three-day right of rescission—if the closing package is signed on Monday, the client has until midnight Thursday to cancel the transaction. The loan will fund on Friday. Saturdays are counted as a rescission day but not a funding day. Sundays and holidays are not counted as either a rescission or funding day. If a closing package for a primary residence refinance is signed on a Thursday, the rescission days are Friday, Saturday, and Monday. The loan will fund on Tuesday. **There is no rescission period for refinancing an investment property.**

The reason interest is collected for the remainder of the month at closing is because mortgage payments are paid in arrears, unlike rent which is paid in advance. If the purchase loan closes August 25, interest is collected from August 25 through August 31. The first payment is due October 1, which pays the September principal and interest.

Some lenders allow **interest credits**, if the loan closes during the first part of the month (usually by the tenth). If the purchase loan closes August 5, rather than collecting interest from the client for the fifth through the thirty-first, the lender credits the client with five days of interest on the settlement statement. Then, the first payment would be due September 1, paying the August principal and interest in its entirety. This allows clients with limited funds to reduce the money required to bring to closing. Ask the lender's closing department if interest credits are allowed, and if so, what day of the month the loan must fund to qualify. A lot of lenders don't allow interest credits.

Since interest begins accruing on the day the loan funds, using an interest credit doesn't cost more or less than the traditional method of paying the month's interest at closing. The only difference is when the money is paid at funding, with the next payment due thirty days from the first of the next month or the first of the next month. Some buyers have a hard time coming up with funds to close, so interest credits can help a buyer come to the closing with less money.

Homeowner's Insurance is a prepaid expense collected at closing. On purchases, the entire annual premium is collected, plus two or three months' premiums for the cushion. For refinances, the amount collected will be a function of how many payments will be made on this transaction until the premium is due. The difference is collected at closing, plus the cushion.

Title charges are fees from the attorney and/or title company. Ask the attorneys and title companies you use most to provide generic fees to input in the GFE. Keep in mind these fees will change if the closing becomes more complex. Be sure to ask about the charge to close a second mortgage in conjunction with a first. There will always be a second set of recording fees. Most attorneys and title companies will also charge a fee for closing the second.

Recording fees are fees charged to record the new mortgage and deed on purchases (mortgage only on refinances unless the names on the deed change) at the probate judge's office. Many states also collect tax stamps. Check with your attorney or probate judge's office to find out what fees are collected and how to calculate them. They are generally charged by the loan amount or number of pages of the documents.

Truth-In-Lending

The Truth-In-Lending (TIL) disclosure shows the client the cost of the loan considering both interest rate and lender fees. The cost is reflected as an Annual Percentage Rate (APR). Many clients confuse the APR with the interest rate on the note. APR will equal the note rate only when there are no lender fees or in the years after the initial transaction. To calculate APR, the interest rate, repayment period, loan amount and lender fees are required. Your application software will calculate the APR, however, you must identify the lender fees that affect the APR by marking them on the GFE as Prepaid Finance Charges (PFC). Review settlement statements from closed loans with a particular lender or ask the closing department to make sure you have all costs/fees affecting the APR marked correctly.

Another confusing aspect of the Truth-In-Lending disclosure is that the amount financed is less than the loan amount. The difference is the lender fees. The rationale is if a lender gives you "X" amount of money on a loan, and you give them "Y" amount in closing costs, you really only received the money listed in the Amount Financed block. This notice is for disclosure purposes only. The loan amount will be the amount on the 1003.

If the program has an adjustable rate, enter the information on the TIL.

Demand Feature. Most notes include a demand feature; which "demands" the entire remaining balance on the loan be paid in full if payments have not been made on time. This feature is part of the foreclosure procedure. If the loan is not paid in full, the lender will foreclose on the property. If the note is paid as scheduled, the demand feature cannot be exercised.

Late Charge. Usually 5 percent of the payment amount if the loan payment is more than fifteen days late. Incurring a late charge will not necessarily adversely affect the client's credit rating on the credit report. The late charge applies if the payment is more than fifteen days late. A late payment is reported on the credit report if the payment is more than thirty days late.

Review the terms of the particular loan program to determine if there is a prepayment penalty.

Most programs do not allow a refund of the finance charge (interest) if the loan is paid off early. This is because most programs have payments that pay interest that has already accrued in the past. Interest is not collected in advance. Remember, the first due date after closing pays the previous month's principal and interest.

Most programs do not allow a new buyer to assume an existing loan from the current owner.

Always check the last two boxes indicating that the numbers are estimates.

Other Disclosures

There are many other disclosures required to be given to the client, with a signed copy in your package. Many are standard, such as an authorization to obtain a credit report, verifications of deposit, employment, and other information. **Other disclosures are required by various states and lenders. Check with your state regulating agency to determine disclosures you are required to give the client.**

Following are the basic disclosures.

- Information booklet explaining closing costs. (***Must be given to the client within three days of the original application on purchase transactions, per RESPA.***)

- Authorization to obtain information, including ordering a credit report

- Privacy policy (broker)

- Client may select the attorney/title company and appraiser as long as the lender approves

- Broker Agreement that details broker charges and fees and state that the client is under no obligation to close the loan with the broker

- Disclosure of any business relationships your company has with a third party in this transaction. (Example: your company has an ownership interest in the appraisal or credit report company.)

- Servicing Disclosure—states the lender has the right to sell the loan and the percentage of loans sold in the past

- Right of the client to receive a copy of the appraisal

- Flood Zone Notification—if the property is in a flood zone, the client must obtain flood insurance

- Equal Credit Opportunity—no discrimination in making loans

- Federal Fair Lending Notice

- Upfront fees—credit report and appraisal

- Consumer handbook on adjustable rate mortgages (if applicable) have been given to the client

Most disclosures may be generated in your application software or provided by the lender or the state. Check with your state and lenders for other required disclosures.

CHAPTER 8

Selecting the Loan Program

Selecting the appropriate loan program is crucial to underwriting approval and client satisfaction. The client should be able to give you a general idea about their priorities and circumstances. If the client needs help selecting the best loan program to fit their requirements and you are not sure of the correct choice, check with your account executives representing your different lenders. The account executives should also be able to tell you about any special or unique program requirements. Also, most lender web sites have options to let you input the loan parameters to find all applicable programs. The more you work with a program, the more familiar you will become with the guidelines and restrictions. Programs and guidelines can change at any time so be aware of any new developments. Generally, your account executives should keep you up to date on any changes. Also, lender web sites should publish notices of any relevant program changes. Some lenders allow you to speak to underwriters directly with program/underwriting questions. The more information you have about the client's situation, the easier it will be to select the appropriate loan program. The better you do selecting the loan program, the faster your file will go through underwriting.

When selecting a loan program, assess the client's situation including:

- Credit Score

- Down payment availability (for purchases)

- Ability to document income

- Assets

- Debt ratio

- Length of time the client plans to be in the property (planning to sell within five years may indicate an adjustable rate fixed for five or seven years is more appropriate if the initial interest rate is lower than current fixed rates)

- Primary residence or investment (cash flow and property management issues)

Basic Program Requirements

Basic programs under Fannie Mae or Freddie Mac guidelines should have the same general guidelines regardless of the lender.

Full Income/Asset documentation—These loan programs have the lowest interest rates, may be fixed or adjustable rates and have varying repayment periods. Both income and assets must be fully documented. Income stipulates two years' history with a verification of employment or W2s and latest pay stubs. Prior to releasing the closing package, many lenders perform a verbal verification of employment to ensure the borrower is still employed.

Stated Income (documented assets)—Income is stated on the 1003 but not documented. As long as the income is reasonable given the job, the underwriter won't question it. Since assets are documented, make sure any bank statements or other assets used do not show income, including direct deposit of pay. If so, mark out the dollar amount. Documenting income—**having income show up on any bank statement or tax return, even inadvertently, on a stated income program is grounds for the loan to be declined.** Employment is verified.

Remember, stated income programs ARE NOT designed to get your client approved for a loan they can't afford. The stated income programs recognize some income, especially in the case of a self-employed client, cannot be documented under Fannie Mae/Freddie Mac guidelines. When you use these programs, you can count actual income, just don't make up income! That is fraud!

Stated Income/Stated Assets (SISA)—Income and assets are stated on the 1003 but not verified. Employment is verified. These programs have higher interest rates. Note: Fannie Mae and Freddie Mac no longer purchase SISA loans.

Self-Employed Clients—To qualify a self-employed client, regardless of income documentation, you must document that the client has been self-employed for at least two years. Acceptable documentation includes:

- Two years business license

- Two years professional license

- Two years Schedule C from IRS form 1040 (*Remember, if the client is on a stated income program, mark out all income and expenses before submission!*)

- Two years Schedule K from IRS form 1040

Interest Only—These programs allow the client to pay interest only, no principal, for a specified period. After the initial interest only period, the payment will be fully amortized with principal and interest payments due. Although the payment will be somewhat lower than a fully amortized principal and interest payment, the amount of a fully amortized payment applied to principal is small during the early years of the program. There will not be a huge reduction in the payment amount for the interest-only programs.

Pay Option—This program was designed specifically for clients with income that varies throughout the year or seasonal investment property income. Each month the client is offered four payment options: 1) fully amortized thirty-year principal and interest payment, 2) fully amortized fifteen-year principal and interest payment 3) interest only payment, and 4) a minimum payment similar to the minimum payment due on a credit card. The theory behind these options is the client pays fully amortized payments during the months his income is high, or his investment property is fully rented, but has smaller payments during the periods of lower income or empty investment property. The problem with this program arises if the client always pays only the minimum payment due, which will lead to negative amortization (owing more than the value of the property). With each minimum payment, the principal is not reduced AND the interest accrued may not be fully paid. The unpaid interest is added to the principal balance. Over a period of time, the client could put himself in a position of negative amortization, especially in a declining real estate market. Although these programs are recast (reevaluated) every few years, there is still a potential for the client to be in a position of negative amortization. I did not offer these programs unless someone specifically asked for them. I would qualify them based on the fully amortized loan payments.

<u>VA</u>—Lenders to qualified veterans are guaranteed repayment by the Veteran's Administration. Borrowers must qualify on credit, debt ratio, and income for lender programs. No down payment is required.

<u>FHA</u>—Loans are guaranteed by the Federal Housing Administration. FHA programs are primarily for low-to-moderate income clients or first-time home buyers with little credit history and a small down payment amount.

Down Payment

The lowest rate programs usually require a down payment of a minimum of 5 percent of the sales price. The funds have to be sourced (documented that the money is from an approved source) and seasoned (in the client's account for at least sixty days). If the money has been in the client's account for sixty days, the money is considered to be sourced and seasoned. Any large deposits must be documented (sourced).

Tax refunds are considered sourced and seasoned.

Equity from the sale of the current residence is a valid source of funds for the down payment and closing costs of this transaction. The settlement statement from the sale of the current residence will be required to document the amount of money the client receives. Because the sale of the current residence is often within a day, or even the same day as closing this transaction, the underwriter will make the settlement statement on the sale of the current residence as a Prior to Funding condition, allowing you to order the closing package, rather than making it a Prior to Documents condition.

Gifts from immediate family members are possible on most programs. The 3 percent down programs allow the entire 3 percent down payment to be a gift. On the conforming programs, the client may use a gift for a down payment, but the client must have 5 percent of his own funds in the transaction. EXCEPTION: When the gift is at least 20 percent of the sales price, the client is not required to have his own funds in the transaction. Documentation required for monetary gifts used as a down payment include a gift letter (Exhibit 3) and sometimes asset documentation showing the relative had the money to give.

VA loans have relatively low rates but do not require a down payment. Other no down payment programs generally have higher rates than those requiring a down payment.

Reducing the Amount of Funds to Close

Most programs require that the funds to close be sourced and seasoned (generally, the money must be in the client's account for sixty days, hence the requirement for two month's statements on the accounts).

Tip: If the client is having a hard time coming up with sourced and seasoned funds to close a purchase, he should consider paying the first year's homeowner's insurance premium directly to the agent. The agent will send the insurance declarations page, along with the paid invoice, to the processor and the attorney. The settlement statement will show the premium as a POC item (Paid Outside of Closing) and will generally not require further documentation.

Earnest money is not usually sourced or seasoned. A larger earnest money payment, given when the contract is signed as "consideration," means less money the client must bring to closing. The amount of earnest money paid must be documented, either by front and back copies of the cancelled check or a statement on the realtor's letterhead that the money was received, if the amount is greater than 2 percent of the sales price. Of course, the underwriter may ask for documentation of the earnest money payment as a condition for closing. Earnest money paid, which is less than 2 percent of the sales price is generally not documented.

Closing at the end of the month will save several hundred dollars in prepaid interest.

If the client must close at the beginning of the month, find out if the lender allows interest credits. Many do not. This will eliminate the prepaid interest the client must pay at closing. If allowed, the interest credit applies to loans funded by a certain date—usually the tenth of the month. Rather than collecting interest from the client from the date of closing through the end of the month, the lender credits the client for the interest from the first of the month through the closing/funding date. The first payment is due on the first of the next month, paying the entire interest due on the previous month. Example: If the purchase loan closes the fifth of August, rather than collecting interest from the client for the fifth through the thirty-first, the lender credits the client five days of interest on the settlement statements. Then, the first payment would be due September 1, paying August principal and interest in its entirety.

Purchasing a Property Owned by a Relative

When a relative owns the property that the client wants to buy, the relative may give the client a gift of equity—the difference between the sales price and the appraised value, to be used instead of a down payment. No cash is involved in the gift of equity, and the transaction is treated similar to a rate/term refinance. The loan-to-value is based on the appraised value rather than the sales price. The relative must submit a letter stating the nature of their relationship to the client and the equity is a gift with no repayment required. Most programs require the client to have at least 5 percent of his own funds in the transaction unless the gift of equity is 20 percent or more of the sales price.

An alternative to a purchase with a gift of equity is adding the client to the deed, and then having the client refinance on a cash-out transaction, paying the relative the amount of money required. The advantages are taking advantage of the property's equity, no down payment (usually), and the ability to roll in closing costs. There will be attorney and recording fees to add the client to the deed, but that will be offset by the savings to the client by refinancing rather than purchasing. There will be a three-day right of rescission if the client will be living in the property.

Some loan programs have no "seasoning" requirements; once the deed is recorded, you can proceed with the cash-out refinance. Other lenders require a period of time before the client is allowed to refinance after being added to the deed. Check the lender and loan program for seasoning requirements.

Bridge Loans

Clients who want to purchase a new home before they sell their former home frequently ask about bridge loans. These programs have higher interest rates and are only necessary in extreme circumstances (high debt ratio, must move and purchase immediately). A bridge loan allows the client to pull the equity out of his existing home for the down payment on the new home, with only one mortgage payment for the next six months.

The bridge loan refinances the current home's mortgage(s) plus cash out for the down payment on the new home. Interest is prepaid for six months at funding, so no payments will be due for six months. The client takes enough cash out for the down payment on his new home. (**NOTE: The cash out MUST be used as a down payment on the new home.**) The bridge loan lender finances the new home. The client must make regular payments on the loan for the new home. The client has six months to sell his current home and pay off the bridge loan. If the home has not sold in six months, he pays interest only payments for the next six months. Most bridge loans must be paid off within twelve months.

Rates and fees on both loans—the refinance of the current home and the financing for the new home—are generally higher than could be found otherwise.

An Alternative to Bridge Loans

The equity in the current home is an acceptable down payment source for the new home financing. A Home Equity Line of Credit on the existing residence is a quick and easy way to pull the equity out of the current home and qualify for the lowest rate programs with 5 percent down on the purchase of the new home. Many HELOCs have no closing costs. Most require that the loan be open for three years or closing costs (usually only a few hundred dollars) must be repaid. However, some lenders will waive closing costs if the HELOC is closed due to the sale of the subject property. They will also generally waive the closing costs if a HELOC is opened on the new home, perhaps to avoid Private Mortgage Insurance by keeping the first mortgage at 80 percent of the purchase price.

We developed a relationship with a local bank with good rates and terms which would close the loans within a couple of days. We would provide the application package on the purchase transaction, which would save the HELOC lender several days of work.

If you are using a HELOC on the current home as the source of the down payment, remember to add the payment in the debt ratio, along with the existing first mortgage payment on the current residence, when you are getting the loan approved. Also, provide the documentation on the rate, terms, and payments in your application package for the underwriter to review. Underwriters will usually require a copy of the note and the mortgage as documentation.

CHAPTER 9

Loan Approval

Either applications can be uploaded directly, or they can be manually entered into the lender's web site for approval. Each lender approval method is different, so it may take awhile to get used to the various systems. Be aware that most systems have quirks that can be difficult to work around the first time. Patience, logical thinking, and help from technical support will usually get you past the problems. Be sure to make good notes when you resolve a system problem so you will be ready when it comes up again!

Review the application for accuracy and completeness prior to uploading into the lender's approval system.

Once the application is uploaded into the lender's system and the approval is obtained, you should have access to the client's credit report. The report should be reviewed against the original application. Revise the application to reflect the debt shown on the credit report, including lender, remaining loan amount, and payment amount. Once you have revised the liabilities section of the application, **RERUN THE APPROVAL! NEVER issue an approval letter based on client-supplied liability information! If the approval is for a full-income documentation program, make sure you have the required income documentation for income reflected on**

the application (1003) prior to running the approval and issuing the approval letter.

The **approval letter** (Exhibit 4) should contain a statement indicating the loan approval is subject to no changes in the client's income, debt, or credit rating and the appraised value of the property.

Some clients will obtain a generic approval letter prior to searching for a home that states how much they can borrow to assure their realtor they can obtain financing. These letters should state the amount for which the client will qualify. The realtor should keep this letter confidential. Most contracts require that the client obtains a loan approval within a specified number of days. For contract required approval letters, I recommend that a dollar amount is NOT included in the approval letter because that can affect the price negotiations. Normally we would tell the realtor the price range for which the client could be approved. Once a property was found, we would issue a letter to be released to the listing agent saying the client had been approved to purchase the property at a specific address.

On purchases with realtors involved, contact the realtors after the approval to introduce yourself and inform them of your client's loan approval. Be sure to discuss any documentation required that you may need their help on as well as identify any issues that may impact the closing. (Example: The subject property is part of an estate with the heirs living in distant parts of the country so getting the deed signed may take longer than usual.)

Realtors, buyers and sellers do not like to be told you cannot fund by the contract closing date, so be sure to bring up any issues as soon as you are aware of them. Most realtors will be glad to help you any way they can.

If the Loan is Declined

If the loan is declined, review the application information that was input into the lender's system. Sometimes the decline is due to data entry errors or technical problems. Check the debt ratio listed on the disapproval. **One common mistake is transposing liability payments and balances.** Using loan balances to calculate debt ratio will usually guarantee disapproval!

If you cannot get an approval for your client on any loan program that your lenders offer, you must inform your client in writing. If you submit the application to several lenders or programs for approval and some are declined, you do not have to send the client a letter saying the loan was declined if you find a program that will approve him. Most application/processing software programs have a form letter. You should call your client to discuss these options before you send the letter.

CHAPTER 10

Quoting and Locking an Interest Rate

You should be able to lock the loan once it is in the lender's system. Lenders have different policies on locking loans, but no lender wants locked loans that don't fund. Some lenders will penalize brokers if they lock too many loans that never fund. Many clients apply with several brokers/lenders, locking whenever/wherever they can. I would not lock a loan for a client until I was relatively sure he wasn't still shopping around. Sometimes this cost me the deal, but I found those clients who were not loyal were just as likely to pull the loan at the end to go with someone else, wasting all the time, effort, and expense I had put into the file. Once a client has paid for the appraisal, I would assume they were intending to let us broker the loan. This turned out to be true about 95 percent of the time, so it seems to be a good indicator.

When quoting a rate, be sure to review all the lender add-ons that may affect the rate. Most lender web sites have functions that will do this for you, but you should still know how to calculate a rate yourself. Add-ons may apply for loan size, cash-out refinances, not collecting escrows, existing or new second mortgages, investment property, and extended lock periods.

Points and Yield Spread expressed in eighths of a point
Conventional Conforming Thirty-Year Fixed

Rate	15-Day	30-Day	45-Day	60-Day
5.500%	1.625%	1.750%	1.875%	2.000%
5.625%	-0.25%	-0.125%	0.000%	0.125%
5.750%	-0.500%	-0.375%	-0.250%	-0.125%
5.875%	-0.750%	-0.625%	-0.500%	-0.375%
6.000%	-0.875%	-0.750%	-0.625%	-0.500%
6.125%	-1.500%	-1.375%	-1.250%	-1.125%
6.250%	-2.000%	-1.875%	-1.750%	-1.625%
6.375%	-2.250%	-2.125%	-2.000%	-1.875%
6.500%	-2.750%	-2.625%	-2.500%	-2.375%
6.625%	-3.250%	-3.125%	-3.000%	-2.875%
6.750%	-3.750%	-3.625%	-3.500%	-3.375%

Points and Yield Spread expressed as percentages
Conventional Conforming 30 Year Fixed

Rate	15-Day	30-Day	45-Day	60-Day
5.500%	98.2690	98.2060	98.0810	97.9560
5.625%	98.8790	98.8160	98.6910	98.5660
5.750%	99.2900	99.2270	99.1020	98.9770
5.875%	99.8900	99.8270	99.7020	99.5770
6.000%	100.5450	100.4820	100.3570	100.2320
6.125%	101.0660	101.0030	100.8780	100.7530
6.250%	101.5400	101.4770	101.3520	101.2270
6.375%	101.9730	101.9100	101.7850	101.6600
6.500%	102.2040	102.1410	102.0160	101.8910
6.625%	102.6170	102.5540	102.4290	102.3040

Lenders will usually quote rates with yield spread/points listed in increments of eighths of a point with 0.00 at par or basis points with 100.00 at par.

Using the first rate sheet example above, the rate closest to par on a thirty-day lock with no add-ons is 5.625 percent which pays a yield spread of .125 percent. Dropping the rate to 5.5 percent causes the client to pay points (1.75 percent) to get that rate. An add-on of 25 percent for no escrows would require a rate of 5.7 percent.

Using the second rate sheet example above, the rate closest to par on a thirty-day lock with no add-ons is 6 percent which pays a yield spread of .482 percent. Dropping the rate to 5.875 percent causes the client to pay points (.173 percent) to get that rate. The yield spread for the 6 percent rate could absorb a 25 percent add-on for no escrows.

When locking a loan, make sure you lock for a long enough period of time. You should consider time to process (including any known delays such as waiting for payoffs or tracking heirs to sign a new deed), underwriting turnaround time, contract specifications if a purchase, and rescission period for a refinance.

Yield spread, or the amount of money paid "on the back" above the par rate is a sensitive issue. Usually, the broker gets paid the yield spread, although it can be credited to the client and applied to closing costs. Some brokers have used this as an opportunity to get paid significantly more than the 1 percent origination fee and don't always disclose this to the client. Lender and broker fees must be disclosed. As you can see by the rate charts above, it is difficult, or impossible to hit a par rate on loans most of the time. When quoting a rate for a client, make sure you have considered all the add-ons applicable to the specific transaction. The yield spread can help offset your extra costs and expenses that haven't been passed to the client. The yield spread can be collected in lieu of an origination fee or a combination of lower origination fee plus yield spread. The problem with collecting yield spread is not disclosing to the client that it is part of your compensation. There is a use to the client for yield spread. When the client can't pay closing costs and the closing costs can't be rolled into the loan, yield spread can be used to pay closing costs, usually applied as a broker credit.

CHAPTER 11

Reviewing the Credit Report

Once the initial approval is obtained through the lender's web site, you should be able to review the credit report. The report usually includes information from all three bureaus—Trans Union, Equifax, and Experian. The easiest reports to read are the "tri-merged" which lists information from all bureaus by credit item. The other report will spit out information by bureau so you will see the same credit account three times (six times if there is a co-borrower with the same credit accounts!).

The beginning of the credit report should list public records, which include bankruptcies, tax liens, and judgments. Look for any adverse information that may affect your approval. If you see something that you weren't expecting, check with the client to determine if the information is accurate. You may be dealing with a case of identity theft, or the client may have either forgotten or failed to disclose adverse information, thinking you won't find out.

If the client has had a bankruptcy, the underwriter will usually require a copy of the complete set of bankruptcy papers. Lenders and programs vary depending upon how far back the bankruptcy occurred before requiring the papers. Check with your underwriter.

Each bureau will issue a credit score based upon proprietary formulas considering payment history, amount of debt, how close balances are to card limits, account age, etc. Credit scores range from 300 to 850. Most creditors report to the three major bureaus—Experian, TransUnion, and Equifax. Most lenders use the numerical middle score to evaluate credit. To qualify for the lowest rate lenders, the client should have at least a 620-630. Credit scores over 700 will qualify for most any program offered, usually with reduced documentation requirements.

To qualify for a mortgage loan, the client should have at least three trade lines opened for a year, with a high balance of at least $1,000.00.

Each trade line will contain information about the account, including type of account (mortgage, installment, or revolving) high balance, current balance, payment history, and if the client is the borrower or co-borrower.

Go through the report, highlighting open accounts. Make a list indicating creditor name, account number, balance and payment amount. This will make it a lot easier to update the 1003. After correcting the liabilities section on the 1003, be sure to re-run the approval with the correct debts.

Most clients don't remember to list every creditor, especially if they have a lot of debt or the debt is small. If there is a discrepancy, be sure to discuss it with the client to make sure the debt is theirs. In addition, if the client has multiple mortgages from investment properties, you should ask which mortgage goes with which properties. Note the property address for each mortgage on the liability section of the 1003, as well as on the credit report. The 1003 will be more accurate and the underwriter will thank you for this.

If two (or more) unmarried co-borrowers are on the loan, each must have a separate credit report run. Joint reports are for married couples only. If you have unmarried co- borrowers, be sure to collect the credit report fee from each applicant.

Understanding and Calculating Debt Ratios

A debt ratio is total monthly payments divided by GROSS monthly income. Debts included are mortgage payments including taxes and insurance, credit card minimum payments, car payments, and other consumer loan payments. For credit cards, use the minimum payment due, not the amount the client actually pays. Utility bills, phone bills, cell phone bills, and insurance payments are not counted in the debt ratio. If it shows up on the credit report, it should usually be included in the debt ratio. Most of the lowest rate programs will allow up to 40 percent debt ratio. Loans will be approved with higher ratios if credit scores are high (over 700) and/or the client has a lot of assets documented. I have seen loans approved with 70 percent to 80 percent debt ratio. An underwriter told me he had seen a loan approved with a 90 percent debt ratio. Most loans will not be approved with high debt ratios.

CHAPTER 12

Verifications

Verification forms, found in the application software, may be used in lieu of other documentation from the client or the credit report.

Verification of Deposit (VOD) may be used instead of two month's bank statements.

Verification of Rent or Mortgage (VOR/VOM) may be used if the liability is not reported on the credit report and the client does not have cancelled checks to document on-time payments. If the landlord/mortgage holder is an individual, the underwriter may not accept the VOR/VOM. A Verification of Rent or Mortgage from a property management company or lender is acceptable. Most program guidelines do not allow VOR/VOMs from individuals.

Verification of Loan (VOL) is required from a creditor when the debt is not on the credit report.

Verification of Employment (VOE) replaces the W2 and pay stub.

The verifications must be completed by the appropriate authority and it must list the contact information. Most underwriters will now

Cheryl L. Peck

accept copies rather than forms with original signatures. **Under no circumstances should the client transport or otherwise handle the verifications.** Remember to verify business numbers through the phone book or the Internet.

CHAPTER 13

The Real Estate Sales Contract

The sales contract is a written agreement between the buyer(s) and seller(s) detailing the terms of the sale. One of the documents usually signed at closing is an affidavit stating that the terms of the contract have been fully met with the closing and there are no other outside agreements. The underwriter will review the terms of the contract in relation to the loan program guidelines.

On purchases, request the contract as soon as possible. Review the sales contract to ensure it meets the program guidelines. This accelerates the underwriting process and avoids delays that may hinder the closing. Many times this means you will work with a contract that is not "fully executed" or signed by both buyer and seller. As long as the terms of the contract have been substantially agreed upon, you don't need a fully executed contract until the file is submitted to underwriting. If there is a delay in receiving a fully executed contract, and if perhaps the seller lives out of town, the underwriter may issue a conditional approval and require the fully executed contract prior to ordering the closing package (PTD condition).

Buyers' Names. Check the buyers' names on the contract both at the beginning of the contract and the signatures to make sure they agree with the names/format on your application. Many underwriters will require that the names appear exactly as they will be shown on the application, deed, and mortgage.

<u>Closing Costs</u>. Make sure the amount of the seller paid closing costs are within the program's guidelines. On most Fannie Mae/Freddie Mac programs, the seller may pay up to 3 percent of the sales price in buyer's closing costs and prepaids. *If the property will be non-owner-occupied, the seller contributions to closing is limited to 2 percent.* To apply any of the seller paid closing costs to prepaids (buyer's interest and homeowners insurance premium), the contract must state "closing costs and prepaids." Otherwise, the money will be applied to closing costs only. Any leftover amount goes back to the seller. The seller-paid closing costs are usually built into the price of the house and are subtracted from the proceeds (loan amount plus down payment) with the seller receiving the net amount. Usually the seller will not bring money to the closing (some sellers are unclear about this). If the sales price is not enough to pay off the existing liens, plus closing costs, someone must bring cash to the closing for the closing costs. I always suggested that if the buyer was asking the seller to pay all or part of the closing costs, the dollar amount was listed. (Example: Seller will pay up to $3,500.00 in closing costs and prepaids.) Stating a limit on the amount the seller will pay helps the seller feel comfortable that he will not be stuck paying an amount higher than expected once he gets to closing.

Tip: Suggest that any seller-paid closing costs in the contract be listed as a dollar amount to assure the seller he will be paying what he expects to pay at closing.

<u>Closing Date</u>. Check the closing date to make sure it is reasonable. If there is any situation that may delay closing, address it as soon as possible to the buyer and realtors. No one wants to find out the day before the contract specified closing date that they won't be closing.

<u>**Time is of the Essence**</u>. This harmless-sounding phrase can cause a tremendous amount of stress and threats of lawsuits. "Time is of the essence" is a legal term that refers to the date of closing and possession. If the sale must be closed on or before January 31, and "Time is of the Essence" is marked "Yes," on February 1, the contract is null and void unless both parties agree to reinstate it. If "Time is of the Essence" is marked "No" and closing takes place a few days later, most reasonable people would consider the contract still valid. (A closing five or six months later would not be reasonable, of course.)

I had a situation early in my career that emphasized the importance of this little phrase. My client was self-employed and had credit issues. It took longer than usual to get everything processed and approved. The contract said the closing must take place by January 31, and time was of the essence. January 31 was on a Saturday. On Thursday, January 29, we were waiting for the final Prior to Documents condition—documentation from the IRS that the client had paid overdue taxes (which he finally paid on Thursday, January 29). By the time the IRS faxed the required documentation it was after 6:00 p.m. The underwriter couldn't review the documentation until Friday (January 30) morning. By the time the file had received final approval and was ready to close, it was too late to get a package to the attorney by the close of business on Friday (this was before the evolution of e-mailed closing packages; the original had to be sent by overnight delivery to the attorney). We could close Monday, February 2, the next business day. The seller refused and cancelled the contract. I suspect he had another buyer willing to pay a higher sales price; otherwise, it didn't make any sense to lose the sale. My client was furious and consulted an attorney to sue the seller. The attorney explained that given the "Time is of the Essence" provision in the contract, the seller was within his rights and it would be futile to sue. The moral of the story is to always check to see if time is of the essence and make sure your client is aware of the ramifications!

Additional Provisions. Many times the contract includes a provision for the buyer to obtain a home inspection. If so, coordinate with the buyer or realtors to determine when the inspection will be completed and reviewed so you can proceed with processing the file efficiently. Under normal circumstances, you should wait to order the appraisal until after an acceptable inspection report has been received by the client.

If the additional provisions list personal property that is included in the sale, it must be removed or listed "at no value." Some underwriters will require that the reference to "personal property be removed completely" or the file will be underwritten with a reduced sales price. This means the client will have to make a larger down payment to make up the difference between the sale price as underwritten and the contract sale price. (Examples of personal property included in the sale were a pool table and equipment, swimming pool equipment, other furniture or appliances.) The real estate mortgage lender is financing "real property" so any personal property included in the sale technically reduces the sales price.

An appraiser once gave me an easy definition of real vs. personal property:

> If the item is free-standing or must be unplugged to move it, it is personal property. If the item must be unscrewed, it is real property. An exception to this definition is the stove, which usually just plugs in but is usually included in the sale and not questioned. However, a refrigerator is considered personal property.

Allowances. Many times the contract calls for a carpet allowance or an allowance for repairs or upgrades. An underwriter will disallow these provisions. The work must be completed and paid for at or before closing or the sales price will be reduced by the amount of the allowance. A buyer is not allowed to receive cash at closing from the seller. If repairs or renovations need to be done under the terms of the contract, the appraisal will be done with a value "subject to" the repairs/renovations. The appraiser will have to re-inspect and provide a report with pictures of the completed work prior to closing, which results in an additional charge. (Be sure to note the charge in your file and include it when ordering the closing package.)

"Subject to" Work/Escrow. Any work required in the contract must be completed prior to closing. Most programs/lenders will not fund the loan, allowing the money to be held in an attorney's escrow account while the work is completed. An exception is minor costs of landscaping. If the work is to be done on the structure, it must be completed prior to the closing. The repairs/improvements, or lack of them, affect the value of the house which is the collateral for the loan. Once the loan has been funded, the lender has no way to verify that the work has been completed and there is no recourse if it hasn't.

Seller-Generated Contract Forms

Many times, buyers and sellers who are not using a realtor will generate their own contract from reference books or the Internet. These may be used. If the client has a self-generated contract, review it to make sure it meets underwriting guidelines. I would also discuss the contract terms with both the buyer and the seller to make sure that what the contract stated was what they meant to do. I had a closing where both the buyer and seller were extremely upset because what they stated in the contract was not what they meant to do. The attorney explained that everyone was legally bound to conduct the transaction based on the terms of the contract. The only alternative was to cancel the closing and start over with a new contract. They chose to close but I learned to always let both parties know how the terms they were agreeing to in the contract would affect the closing. If a realtor is involved, they should have a standard contract that he or she will explain to the buyer and seller themselves.

The Inspection

Although not required by the lender, inspections identify problems that may effect the transaction. Even new homes have things wrong with them. Most issues are minor and will be ignored or easily fixed before closing. Some issues, such as structural problems, may be sufficient to cancel the contract. The buyer reviews the inspection, evaluating the seriousness of each issue. The buyer may ignore the issue, request that the seller repair/replace the item prior to closing, renegotiate the sales price, or cancel the contract and receive a refund of the earnest money.

You are not responsible for ordering the inspection. The client or selling agent will do this. You do not have to include a copy of the inspection in the application package submitted to the underwriter.

If the buyer is getting an inspection, do not order the appraisal until the buyer has a chance to review and accepts the inspection report. Once the appraisal is completed, you owe the fee. If the transaction is cancelled due to the inspection results, your client (or you) has paid for an appraisal that they cannot use.

Sometimes the buyer will be in a hurry to close and feels confident that the house is in good shape so they want the appraisal completed concurrently with the inspection. Make sure you know the buyer's wishes before you proceed.

CHAPTER 14

Ordering Appraisal, Title Work, and Insurance

The Appraisal

Always review the approval notice to determine what type, if any, appraisal is required. Most will require full appraisals. If the credit score is extremely high and the loan-to-value is extremely low, some lenders will waive the appraisal requirement, usually charging a fee that is a lot less than the cost of an appraisal. Make sure you have the client's permission before you actually place the order. Sometimes issues come up—especially on purchases—and the client changes his mind about the transaction. Don't spend the client's money unless he approves! Have the client or realtor, give you the name, and phone number of the person to be contacted for entry into the property. Sometimes clients want to be present during the appraisal. If so, note fact that on the request form and make sure the appraiser informs the client of the appointment.

Your application software should have a request form for ordering the appraisal. The appraiser does not require the inspection report. Fax or e-mail the completed form, along with the sales contract on a purchase to the appraiser. For refinances, fax or e-mail the request form along with the deed. Most lenders require a copy of the appraiser's license in the application package, so be sure to remind the appraiser to include the license with the report. On refinances, I always included the amount the client expected his home to appraise for on the order. If the appraiser saw this amount was out of line with the comparable sales in the neighborhood, he would let us know so we could discuss the issue with the client before proceeding. Some clients have an inflated idea of the value of their property. If the property will not appraise high enough to meet the purpose of the refinance, especially on cash out transactions, we could stop the appraisal order before the client's money was spent.

Tip: Always tell the appraiser what the refinance client expects his home to appraise for (purchases will be based on the contract) and ask him to tell you if the comparables won't support it before he does the inspection.

Some lenders require that the appraiser be on an approved appraisers list. Adding an appraiser to the list is usually simple but can hold up closing if you don't find out soon enough. Always check a new lender's appraiser requirements so you can make sure you meet their guidelines.

The appraiser should acknowledge the receipt of your request and should call the Point of Contact, provided by you on the request form, to schedule an appraisal. I always asked the appraiser to call the point of contact within twenty-four hours to schedule the appointment, even if the appointment was several days later. That way everyone knows that the appraiser has received the request. The appraiser should also give you an estimated date for receiving the final report. Usually the appraisal report is e-mailed to you. Make sure your e-mail address is on the request.

When you receive the appraisal, make sure the client's name is correct. Review the comparable sales to determine the date of sale and distance from the subject property. Some lenders have specific limits for comparable sales used for both date of sale and distance. Check to see if the appraiser has noted any problems with the property that must be corrected prior to closing. A common example is a water stain on the ceiling, which indicates a leak. Although the leak has most likely been repaired, the underwriter will probably require a roofer or other professional to inspect the property to ensure the leak has been fixed, resulting in an additional charge to be paid at closing. (*Remember to note the charge in the file and include it when ordering the closing package!*) The inspection report should note any problems he sees but the inspection isn't required and the appraiser usually doesn't see the report. The appraiser will perform a visual inspection but does not check appliances, water pressure, etc.

Check the property zoning and use. Also, check pictures of the street around the subject property as well as any other indication that the property is next to property that is zoned as commercial. Both Fannie Mae and Freddie Mac have guidelines concerning zoning requirements.

Make sure the appraiser has correctly marked either the "as is" or "subject to" box indicating whether the value depends on future improvements. All "subject to" work must be completed prior to closing. The appraiser must re-inspect the property before closing and submit a report with pictures verifying the work has been completed satisfactorily. A re-inspection could delay closing so be sure everyone is aware of the requirement and the date the appraiser re-inspects the property. If the appraisal was an "as is" report, make sure there are no repairs or maintenance required.

New construction in new subdivisions can be a problem. A home sale has to be offered on the open market to be eligible for use as a comparable. Custom home sales contracted between the buyer and the builder cannot be used as a comparable sale in the appraisal report. New subdivisions may not have acceptable comparables. Without comparable sales within the distance specified in the underwriting guidelines, the loan may be declined.

The appraisal will note whether the subject property has been listed for sale within the last twelve months. This is done by reviewing Multiple Listing records, and a property listed For Sale By Owner will probably not show up. *Remember, if a property has been listed for sale within the last twelve months, Fannie Mae/Freddie Mac guidelines will not allow refinance transactions.*

The appraisal will note whether the property is in a flood zone. If so, the buyer needs to be prepared to obtain flood insurance. The underwriting requirement for flood insurance will come from the flood certification report they order right before the file is cleared for closing. Clients who are refinancing should already know if the property is in a flood zone and requires flood insurance.

Make sure the appraisal has been signed and dated correctly. If the appraisal was done by an apprentice, most lenders want the supervising appraiser to have inspected the property himself, so make sure the supervisor has checked that he inspected the property.

Appraisers consider whoever ordered the appraisal to be the client. If you ordered the appraisal, you have control of it. If the client changes broker/ lenders, you have to authorize the transfer of the appraisal. Otherwise, the new broker/lender will have to obtain a new appraisal.

Most lenders allow the appraisal to be e-mailed directly to the underwriter. Once you receive and review the appraisal, a good practice is to immediately forward it to the underwriter, client, and insurance agent (if a purchase). When sending the appraisal to the insurance agent, include the client's loan number, mortgagee clause(s), and projected closing date.

Title Work

The attorney or title company will perform a title search to insure all liens and mortgages are paid and released at closing, which allows the buyer to assume ownership of the property with a clear title. Depending upon the attorney's schedule, this could take several days. A title insurance policy will be issued at closing in the lender's name, which is required by the lender. Owner's coverage is optional, and requires a small additional fee; it should be purchased. Title insurance will protect the lender and/or buyer from losses due to title issues that may be discovered after closing. The owner's title policy will protect the client for as long as he owns the property.

The client will receive the title policy by mail about four weeks after the closing. He should keep it in his real estate file. If he ever refinances, he should take the policy to his mortgage broker to copy and submit it to the closing attorney/title company. This will allow the title company to re-issue the existing policy, rather than writing a new policy, saving approximately 40 percent on the premium. (Note: the title insurance premium is a one-time fee paid at closing.)

If a married client is to be on the loan and deed alone on a primary residence, let the attorney, and underwriter know, and include the spouse's name. There may be documents a spouse must sign at closing.

Purchases. Fax or e-mail a request for title work to the attorney or title company when you receive the appraisal money, along with the contract. (I always used the receipt of the appraisal money as the official "kick-off" for processing the file. Once the appraisal is paid for, you can be reasonably sure the client is serious about completing the transaction with you and the attorney/title company.) You should also make sure the attorney has the contact information for all involved in the transaction, a copy of the sales contract, and insurance declarations page, when available. They will also need the lender's name and address, and loan amount for the title policy and closing protection letter. Second mortgage information should be included, if applicable.

<u>Refinances</u>. When ordering title work for a refinance, submit the request, deed, insurance declarations page, mortgage statement or coupon (to accelerate the process for receiving the payoff), and the title policy, if available. On the request form, be sure to include the mortgagee information and the loan amount. Include second mortgage information, if applicable.

You will receive the title commitment and the closing protection letter. The closing protection letter, issued by the attorney's errors and omissions insurance carrier, states that the lender is protected from mistakes made by the attorney. Both documents should be included in your application package that is submitted to the underwriter.

Note: Remember, the common misconception is that if the seller pays the closing costs they can select the closing attorney. According to RESPA, the buyer selects the closing attorney subject to the lender's approval. No matter which side of the settlement statement closing costs are listed (buyer's or seller's) the paying closing costs are built into the sales price. The attorney actually represents the lender, (who is funding the loan!) and insures all documents are correct, complete, and the contract has been fulfilled. The buyer and seller do not need separate representation. The majority of the closing package consists of disclosures. The main documents are the settlement statement (listing charges/fees), note (lists terms of loan), and mortgage (puts the lien on the property).

Homeowner's Insurance

<u>Refinances</u>. The client should have given you the insurance declarations page for the property during the initial interview, or at least the name and phone number of the agent. The current "Dec" page, which shows the property address, effective dates, coverage and premium amounts, will be enough to submit the file to underwriting. The insurance agent should be notified of the refinance, closing date, new loan number and mortgagee clause, early enough to get you a revised Dec page prior to closing. Some agents require authorization from the client before they will release any information or make changes to the policy. USAA requires client authorization, so be sure to tell a client using USAA insurance to notify them of the refinance, and authorize USAA to talk to you. USAA issues client ID numbers so ask the client for theirs. Once USAA has authorization to disclose the information, you can do everything over the phone and they can fax the revised Dec page immediately while you are on the phone.

<u>Purchases</u>. The client must talk to the insurance agent to determine the specifics of coverage, deduction, and premium. The agent will need a copy of the appraisal, usually by e-mail, and the mortgage information—loan, number, mortgagee clause, and projected closing date.

Note: Most lenders will not allow a deductible greater than $1,000.00.

<u>Flood Insurance</u>. If any part of the property is in a flood zone, the entire property is classified as being in a flood zone. If the property is in a flood zone and flood insurance is required, you must obtain an elevation certificate for the structure, obtained by reviewing an elevation survey, to determine the flood insurance premium. An elevation survey documents how high above the flood plain the structure sits; the higher the structure is above the flood plain, the lower the flood insurance premium. If the structure is above the flood plain, the client can submit the elevation

certificate and report to the Federal Emergency Management Agency (FEMA) to have the property ruled out of a flood zone, eliminating the need for flood insurance. This takes about six months, so it isn't something that can be done before closing. The client would have to obtain the flood insurance, and then cancel it after the ruling is received from FEMA stating the property is outside the flood zone. The client should talk to the lender's customer service department to determine the documentation required to change the flood zone classification. The client should also keep the elevation certificate and FEMA ruling in their real estate file for use when/if they sell the property.

The elevation survey will cost several hundred dollars. In our area, it ranges between $500.00 and $600.00. If you order the survey, you are responsible for paying it. If the loan does not close for some reason, you still owe for the elevation survey (and appraisal and anything else you have ordered!). I suggest you have the client order it or pay you before you order it. The surveyor can submit the invoice with the report and you can pay it at closing, or if the client has paid you, send the check upon receipt of the survey and submit the invoice to the attorney to show as a POC (Paid Outside of Closing) item on the settlement statement.

If an elevation certificate is required to obtain flood insurance prior to closing, make sure everyone involved in the transaction is aware that the time required may affect the closing date. Ask the seller if they have a copy of an elevation certificate. If they currently have flood insurance, then they must have had one at some time, although many do not keep up with the documents. I have obtained elevation certificates from the seller's insurance agent, although they are not required to do this, so ask nicely!

CHAPTER 15

Submitting the File to Underwriting

Once you have all the documentation and disclosures, you can prepare your file for submission to underwriting. Most lenders have a preferred stacking order, which is usually:

- Transmittal Summary (1008), generated by the loan application software

- Loan Approval

- Final Application (1003)

- Initial Application (1003), original submitted and signed by the client

- Credit report/explanations/documentation (payoffs, letters of explanation) if any

- Verification of rent or mortgage form (if not on credit report)

- Income documentation

- o W2s (two years) and pay stubs covering thirty days or

- o Verification of Employment form

- Asset documentation (including gift letter, if applicable)

- o Bank statements covering sixty days or

- o Verification of Deposit form

- Sales Contract (if applicable)

- Appraisal, including appraiser's license

- Insurance Declarations Page

- Homeowners' Association Questionnaire (if applicable)

- Disclosures

Review the file to ensure all information is complete and accurate. Make sure all conditions stated in the initial automated approval are included. The Transmittal Summary (Form 1008) and the final application (Form 1003) should show correct LTV/CLTV, income and liability totals. The client does not need to sign the final 1003 prior to submitting the file to underwriting. He will sign a final 1003 at closing. If there were unusual circumstances, put a letter of explanation to the underwriter at the front of the file. Most underwriters appreciate background information, which may speed up their review process.

Make sure all documentation supporting income and assets are included in the file, as well as any credit explanation.

Check the name(s) and spelling of the borrower, ensuring it is done the same way throughout the file. Make sure all signature dates are entered correctly and within RESPA guidelines.

Most lenders will accept packages submitted electronically, which reduces delays and courier costs.

Working Conditions

Once the underwriter reviews the application package, an approval is issued, with conditions. Conditions will be either PTD (Prior to Documents) or PTF (Prior to Funding). All PTD conditions must be cleared by the underwriter prior to drawing and releasing the closing documents. All PTF conditions must be cleared prior to the release of funds.

Review ALL conditions. Most PTF conditions will be for the closing attorney/title company, but sometimes, there will be some that you must submit.

Many times, condition statements are standard and may not be clear. If you have any questions on conditions, be sure to discuss them with the underwriter to ensure you know exactly what he/she is asking for. It is extremely frustrating for both you and the underwriter to submit and resubmit a condition that you're not clear on and they won't accept! Many times a quick phone call can save a lot of time and aggravation.

If the documentation requested is difficult or impossible to obtain, ask for alternatives that would be acceptable. Be creative. Try to think of any possible documentation that might satisfy the underwriter. Some underwriters are helpful and some won't be able to "think outside the box." It is up to you to save the deal!

Once I was supposed to document the amount of Homeowner's Association Dues for a condo that was not the subject property. The condo was one of several investment properties the client owned. The condo was in another state and the only phone number I had for the association was not answered, including evenings and weekends, and my messages were not resulting in a return call. This condition was the only remaining PTD on a purchase of investment property; the seller was a builder and a realtor was involved. The client was a multi-millionaire with a low debt ratio and had a lot of assets. Everyone was pushing to close and no one could understand why an $84 association dues payment was holding up the entire transaction. Frankly, I didn't either. I finally found a condo listed for sale on a realtor's web site that was two doors down from the one I was interested in. The listing showed the amount of the dues. The underwriter accepted the page from the Multiple Listing Service and cleared the condition.

Most conditions can be electronically submitted. Most underwriters want the conditions to be submitted at once rather than one at a time as you receive them. Put the documents in the order requested by the underwriter. Most lenders have specific procedures for submitting conditions. Check the file on the web site periodically to determine whether the underwriter has "signed off" on the conditions. If the underwriter has not reviewed the conditions in the specified time, be sure to verify the conditions were received.

CHAPTER 16

The Closing Process

Ordering the Closing Package

Once all PTD conditions have been cleared, the file will be sent to the lender's closing department and you can order the closing package. Review the sales contract on purchases to make sure you know what the seller is paying, if any. Make sure insurance premiums, along with attorney and title fees are correct. Most lenders charge a fee to redraw the closing package, which will be required if there are changes to the settlement statement after the closing package has been released.

Review your list of additional charges in the client's file to be sure all extra charges have been included (fee for an appraiser's final inspection, surveys, and bank fees for required documentation such as subordination agreements, etc.).

Review the name(s) and addresses of the borrower and property to make sure they are consistent and spelled correctly. How will the names be listed on the deed (for purchases and some refinances)? Does that comply with the borrower's wishes? Have you indicated whether the borrower is married? If the borrower is married and the spouse is not named on the loan, is the spouse required to sign any documents (usually settlement statement, mortgage, and TIL)? If a spouse's signature is required, make sure everyone is informed and will comply.

Many lenders require the underwriter or closer to perform a verbal verification of employment on all borrowers prior to releasing the closing package. This can hold up the release of the closing package. Make sure the underwriter has good contact information and check to see if there are any problems if the package isn't released when you expected.

Closing

Most clients and realtors have a projected closing date even before you start your work. Usually it is possible to meet the date but you should communicate with everyone throughout the process if anything develops that might delay or prevent the closing. Ideally, the closing package is ordered early enough to give the attorney/title company plenty of time to prepare the package, including the settlement statement. By law (RESPA), the client can require the settlement statement twenty-four hours prior to closing for review. I tried to always do this (unless we were in the middle of a closing emergency!) because it eliminates stress at the closing table. Prior review of the settlement statement by all involved parties also saves time because you can answer questions and correct errors prior to closing. Everyone knows how much money, if any, they're required to bring to the closing early enough to avoid a last minute rush to the bank. The closing packages are electronically transmitted so it is easy to send. Most clients won't care about reviewing the entire package, just the settlement statement. The closing secretary at the attorney's office/title company can send copies to all involved parties.

Some clients insist on reading every page of the closing package. To avoid wasting everyone's time at the closing table, make sure these clients get a copy of their closing package at least twenty-four hours prior to closing.

The attorney or title representative will explain the documents in the closing package to the client(s). The main documents to consider are:

1. Settlement statement, which lists all the charges and fees involved in the transaction and who pays and receives what;

2. Note, which details the terms and conditions of the loan, including loan amount, interest rate, fixed vs. adjustable rate, repayment period and prepayment penalty;

3. Mortgage, which places a lien on the property equal to the loan amount.

The other documents in the closing package are mostly disclosures and affidavits (the client intends to live in the property, all terms of the contract have been fulfilled with this closing, the client will cooperate in correcting errors found after closing, etc.).

On a purchase, the client will receive a copy of the unrecorded deed in the closing package. The deed is the title to the property, showing ownership. Unlike car titles, which are retained by the lender until the loan is paid, the original deed will be sent to the client once it is recorded. Many states have a homestead exemption on property taxes that save the client money if they live in the house. If the purchase is for a primary residence, the client should take the recorded deed to the property tax assessor's office and claim the homestead exemption.

After the Loan Has Closed

You should receive a closing package from the closing attorney/ title company at some point after closing. Each state has different documentation requirements. Usually it is easier for the closing attorney/ title company to provide a copy of the entire package rather than pulling various documents throughout the package to copy for you. Some states require copies of the recorded mortgage, which will not be immediately available. Many closing agents will provide you with a copy of the recorded mortgage but you can usually download it from the probate office's web site. Check with your state regulatory agency to find out how long you must keep client files.

Before the closed loan package is filed, make sure all pertinent information is entered into your database or application software. It's much easier to input information as each loan closes rather than emergency data entry of a year's worth of packages to meet audit/inspection requirements!

Be sure to send thank you notes to your client for their business and the trust and confidence they placed in you. Also, be sure to thank whoever referred the client to you as well as any part of the team (realtor, attorney, etc.) who made your job easier. Remember to ask for referrals!

CHAPTER 17

Dealing with Others Involved in the Transaction

In most purchase transactions, you may not be able to control who you are working with, including realtors, attorneys, title companies, appraisers, and others. Although RESPA mandates that the buyer chooses the attorney/title company, (they usually will leave it up to you) most realtors think they, or the seller if the seller pays closing, gets to choose. In addition, many realtors have their own preferences for attorneys, title companies, and appraisers. Some will insist you use their choices. I have had listing agents in some areas of the states I worked in who insisted they were the ones to order the title work. Unfortunately, they didn't let us know until after we had ordered title work from the attorney selected by the buyer. The key to avoiding these situations is to communicate with everyone involved in the transaction. You will have to evaluate who the realtor wants you to use and whether or not it is worth the trouble to fight for your choices. Your goal is to get the loan closed quickly with the least amount of problems. Believe me, if there are any problems with closing, everyone will blame you, even if you had no say in the selection of your team members! You may have had negative experiences with the realtor's choice of team members. You must weigh potential problems against the probability of future referral business from this realtor.

The key to a successful closing is regular communication with everyone involved, including the client(s), attorney/title company, insurance agents and lender. On a purchase, the seller and up to two realtors will be involved. Sometimes it can seem like a full-time job just to keep everyone informed. E-mail is a quick way to send information to everyone who needs it. Also, if the client is working with a realtor, ask him or her to help communicate with the listing agent and seller. Realtors can also help you by getting required documentation, such as fully executed sales contracts, pest inspection letters, and verification of earnest money. A good realtor is a valuable part of the team who can help you do your job more efficiently.

Make sure that you do your part as you deal with others. Provide accurate information quickly so others can do their jobs, pay invoices promptly, and let everyone know the status of your processing efforts. One of the most important things you can do to build your reputation, as well as your referral business, is to **return phone calls and e-mails!** I received thousands of dollars in extra business because I took the time to return calls. It wasn't always easy. During the refinance boom, it would take me as long as two hours in the evening to return phone calls. However, the payoffs were tremendous! I had many clients over the years tell me I was the only broker or loan officer who called them back. In a highly competitive service business such as the mortgage industry, you can't afford to ignore potential clients.

Tip: ALWAYS return phone calls and e-mails, even if you have to stay late to do it!

Glossary

Adjustable Rate Mortgage (ARM): A mortgage loan in which the interest rate may change at specified periods of time by a pre-determined margin according to a pre-selected index.

Amortization: Gradual debt reduction, based upon installment payments according to the original loan amount, interest rate, and repayment period.

Amortization Schedule: Identifies the amount of principal and interest paid for each payment during the life of the loan.

Annual Percentage Rate (APR): Discloses yield to the lender. APR is the amount, expressed as a percentage of the loan amount that the lender receives, including interest payments and lender fees.

Appraisal: A report by a licensed appraiser, which evaluates the subject property with recent sales of similar properties to determine the value of the subject property.

Appreciation: The increase in a property's value due to improvements and/or current market conditions.

Balloon Mortgage: A mortgage with periodic installments of principal and interest payments for a specified period of time; after which the remaining balance is due. (Example: 30/15 mortgages are amortized over thirty years with the remaining balance due at the end of fifteen years.)

Balloon Payment: The lump sum payment due at the end of the specified period to pay off the mortgage.

Basis Point: One percent of the loan amount; used when quoting yield spread or points paid for the interest rate.

Cap: The maximum amount an adjustable rate mortgage can change at each adjustment period and the life of the loan.

Closing: Finalizing the sales or refinance transaction, including signing the mortgage loan closing package, transferring title to the property from the seller to the buyer (if applicable), and paying all fees.

Closing Costs: Fees incurred to finalize the transaction, including lender fees, attorney/title company fees, recording fees, and prepaid interest and insurance.

Closing Protection Letter (CPL) A letter from the attorney's errors and omissions insurance company stating that the lender is protected from attorney mistakes.

Collateral: Security for a debt. A mortgage places a lien on the subject property as collateral for the loan.

Credit Score: A numerical value given to assess the credit/payment history of an individual. The higher the score the better the credit. Most programs with relatively low rates require scores in the mid-to-upper 600s. Three bureaus report credit scores. Most loan programs use the middle of the three scores for underwriting purposes.

Deed: A legal document showing ownership of real property conveyed by the seller to the buyer. The original recorded deed is held by the owner of the property. It is **NOT** like a car title and held by the lender until the mortgage is paid.

Down Payment: Money paid at closing toward the purchase price of the home. The lowest rate programs require 5 percent of the sales price as a down payment.

Equity: The difference between the fair market value and the mortgage loan amount(s) representing an asset of the owner.

Escrow Account: An account set up by the lender to hold monthly payments of real estate taxes and homeowner's insurance premium payments. The lender pays taxes and insurance from this account when due.

Escrow Payment: The amount of the total monthly mortgage payment (PITI) that is for taxes and insurance (TI).

Fair Market Value: The amount a seller can reasonably expect to sell the property for in an open market.

Fannie Mae: A shareholder-owned company with a federal charter to buy real estate mortgage loans from banks and lenders to maximize the availability of mortgage funds to homeowners. The mortgages back securities that are sold to private investors. This practice allows banks and lenders to clear out their warehouse lines of credit so they have more money available to lend to other homeowners.

Freddie Mac: A program similar to Fannie Mae designed to help those with low or moderate incomes, including first-time home buyers, who obtain mortgage financing through their lenders.

Federal Housing Administration (FHA): A division of the Department of Housing and Urban Development (HUD) guarantees loans to lenders under certain conditions to allow those who may not otherwise qualify for a mortgage to obtain one. The FHA program is primarily for first-time home buyers, with little down payment and higher debt ratios.

Foreclosure: The legal procedure whereby a lender takes possession of the property placed as collateral on the loan by the mortgage due to a default in payments.

Hazard/Homeowners Insurance: Covers damage to or loss of the property. If the property is mortgaged, the lender is listed as the mortgagee on the policy.

Index: The financial instrument that is the basis for the interest rate on an adjustable rate program.

Interest: A finance charge collected in addition to the repayment of principal; the cost of the loan.

Interest Credit: A lender credit for interest from the first day of the month through the funding date. The first payment will be due on the first of the next month.

Loan to Value (LTV): The loan amount divided by the appraised value (or sales price on a purchase). The difference is the equity in the property (or the down payment in a purchase). **CLTV,** Combined Loan to Value includes the second mortgage, if applicable.

Margin: The spread, which when added to the index, determines the interest rate.

Mortgage: The recorded document placing a lien on the property based upon the terms of the note. (The mortgage is not the same as the note.)

Non-Permanent Resident Alien: A non-U,S, citizen temporarily in the United States on a Visa for work or pleasure.

Note: The document that obligates the borrower to repay the loan; detailing the terms including rate, repayment period and prepayment penalty (if any).

Payment Shock: The difference between the new mortgage payment and the current rent or mortgage payment.

PITI: Principal, interest, taxes, insurance; the total mortgage payment with escrows.

Point: One percent of the loan amount.

Prepaid Interest: Interest collected at closing from the funding date through the end of the month because the first payment will be made on the first of the second month to pay the principal and accrued interest for the first full month.

Private Mortgage Insurance (PMI): Coverage provided by a mortgage insurance company to protect the lender from losses incurred if the borrower defaults on the mortgage loan. PMI is usually required if the first mortgage is more than 80 percent of the sales price (purchase) or appraised value (refinance).

Sales Contract: A written document specifying the terms of the sale of real estate between a buyer and seller.

Secondary Financing: Second mortgage that is subordinate to the first mortgage.

Sourced Funds: Documentation showing where the money to close comes from—two months' bank statements will show the money in the borrower's account. Tax refunds and cash from the equity on real property are acceptable sources, among others.

Seasoned Funds: Money that has been in an account at least sixty days is considered the borrower's own funds. If the money came from a loan, sixty days should be enough time for the debt to show on the credit report.

Title Insurance: Covers the insured against title problems; usually obtained at the closing of a purchase. Lender's coverage is mandatory if the property is financed. Owner's coverage is optional, but important to the owner and should be obtained.

Veterans Administration: Guarantees loans for lenders made to qualified veterans or veteran's spouses. The VA will charge a funding fee to the veteran/spouse that replaces private mortgage insurance. The funding fee may be rolled into the loan amount.

Warehouse Lines of Credit: A lender's revolving line of credit from a warehouse that the lender used to fund real estate mortgage loans.

Yield Spread: "Back Points," expressed as a percentage of the loan amount paid to the broker for locking interest rates higher than par.

Exhibit 1

Document Checklist

The following documents will be required to process your loan.

For Purchases

_____ Most current paycheck stub

_____ Previous year's W-2

_____ Two month's bank statements for all accounts

_____ Sales Contract

_____ Landlord's name, address, and phone number (if applicable)

_____ Copy of driver's license (or other picture ID)

For Refinances

_____ Most current paycheck stub

_____ Previous year's W-2

_____ Current mortgage statement(s)

_____ Deed

_____ Homeowner's insurance information

_____ Copy of driver's license (or other picture ID)

_____ Title Insurance Policy (if any)

Submit these documents as required, if they apply to you

_____ Investment property leases

_____ Divorce decree

_____ Bankruptcy papers

_____ Two years' federal tax returns with all schedules

_____ Gift letter

Please include a check for $ _____ payable to _____ for the credit report.

Thank you,

Exhibit 2

Information Sheet

Date _____ Type (Purchase/Refi) _____

Loan Amount _____ Appraised Value _____

Sales Price _____ Down Payment _____

Term _____ Second Mtg? _____ Escrow?_____

Refi: R/T or CO CO Amount _____ Roll in closing?_____

FHA Payoff? _____ Escrow?_____

Second?/HELOC? _____ Leave Open? _____

Rate Add-ons: Loan size _____ CO _____ Second _____

N/O/O _____ Condo _____

Referred by: _____ Special Issues: _____

Selling Agent _____ Company _____

Ph _____ Fax _____ Cell _____

Listing Agent _____ Company _____

Ph _____ Fax _____ Cell _____

Attorney _____ Ph _____ Fax _____

Address _____ Point of Contact _____

Insurance _____ Ph _____ Fax _____

Address _____ Point of Contact _____

Credit Report: Paid: _____ Amount: _____

Ordered _____ Received _____

Appraiser: _____ Ph _____ Fax _____

Amount Collected: _____ Date _____ Ordered _____ Received _____

Additional Orders: _____ Received _____

Additional Charges to be collected at closing

Cheryl L. Peck

Vendor	Amount	Purpose

Exhibit 3

Gift Letter

Date

To Whom It May Concern:

I give _____ (client name), my _____
(relationship: son, daughter, etc.) a gift of $ _____
for the purchase of their home.

The money is a gift and does not have to be repaid.

_____

Signed by relative

Exhibit 4

Approval Letter

(On company letterhead)

Date

To Whom It May Concern:

Mr. and Mrs. John Smith have been approved to purchase 123 Main Street, City, State.

This approval is subject to no changes in income, credit, debt, and the appraised value of the property.

If you have any questions or need additional information, please call.

Thank you,

Bill Jones
Loan Officer

Made in the USA
Coppell, TX
08 June 2020